SPORTS CARS

SPORTS CARS

THE WORLD'S HOTTEST SPORTS CARS IN 500 GREAT PHOTOS

Peter Henshaw

CRESTLINE

This edition first published in 2004 by Crestline, an imprint of MBI Publishing Company, Galtier Plaza, Suite 200, 380 Jackson Street, St. Paul, MN 55101-3885 USA

© Salamander Books Ltd., 2004

An imprint of Chrysalis Books Group plc

Crestline books are also available at discounts in bulk quantity for industrial or sales-promotional use. For details please contact Special Sales Manager at MBI Publishing Company, Galtier Plaza, Suite 200, 380 Jackson Street, St. Paul, MN 55101-3885 USA.

ISBN 0-7603-1995-2

CREDITS
Designer: John Heritage
Editor: Katherine Edelston
Production: Don Campaniello
Reproduction: Anorax Ltd

Printed and bound in Malaysia

Contents

INTRODUCTION

What makes a sports car? Is it image, the lack of a roof, the number of seats, or just get up and go? Or is it simply that sports cars put the driving experience first, that's one thing they certainly all have in common.

Left: Jaguar E-Type Lightweight—the distinction between sports cars and racers was often blurred.

For almost as long as there have been cars, there have been sports cars too. Something that offered that little bit extra in the driving experience, whether it be performance, handling, or simply the wind in the hair.

Above: Handsome is...and handsome does...with the SS100, Jaguar hit on two sports car essentials, good looks and fine performance.

Right: Jaguar SS100. The "Coventry Cat" made its name by applying stylish, sporty bodywork to mundane (and cheap) mechanical parts. The SS100 broke away from that, offering performance too—it was the start of a long Jaguar tradition.

That much we can agree on, but a precise definition of the sports car is less easy.

A lot of people would say that a sports car has two seats, an open top, and a powerful engine mated to a manual transmission. That sounds reasonable enough, until you look a little more closely. Stick to that definition like a zealot, and you'd have to discount any number of hard top Ferraris. Or what about the 2+2-seat E-Type Jaguar or the semi-auto transmission Sportomatic Porsches? As for performance, the original Austin-Healey Sprite and Porsche 356 were no tarmac burners, even by the standards of their time. Does that disqualify them from sports car status?

It doesn't of course. All of these are undoubtedly sports cars, as the heart of anything worthy of the term is far more nebulous in character than the number of seats or type of transmission it happens to have. Sports saloons, the GTs, Gtis, and SR brigades, don't have it,

Left: After 1945, the first sports cars on offer were no more than mild updates of pre-war designs. This MG Midget TC, the first British sports car to crack the American market, was typical.

being warmed up versions of cooking family cars. In fact, that is one concrete definition we can use—a sports car has its own unique bodyshell. It may share any number of hidden components with a cheaper saloon (a simple fact of economic life) but it will look quite different. And at the heart of it is the wish to put the driving experience first, or at least higher up the list of priorities.

That driving experience could come in any number of ways. The basic "wind in the hair" appeal of a Morgan or MG, for example, where sheer speed comes second to the joy of being open to the elements. A Mustang or Corvette V8 of the '60s could provide blistering, tire smoking straight-line acceleration of the dragstrip kind. Either of those American pony cars would leave an early Lotus Seven far behind over the standing quarter-mile. But the Lotus, the original four-wheeled motorbike, would soon be out in front on narrow, twisty roads, with its unrivaled quick steering and seat of the pants

handling. Either way, whoever was driving would be enjoying a very intense experience. In its way, the Lotus was quite a sophisticated little car, relying on the genius of Colin Chapman's design skills instead of brute force.

Of course, some people like brute force, and for them, an AC Cobra would provide the sort of wild ride they'd appreciate—unsophisticated, even crude? Perhaps, but

Above left: Not many American manufacturers made a serious attempt at sports car building in the 1950s, but Kaiser was one who did.

Above and right: Early days for two illustrious European marques, just getting into their stride as Kaiser passed away. The Jaguar XK120 (above) carried on the SS100 formula of good performance and stunning looks at a low price. Ferrari (right) wasn't about value for money, but V12 racecars that could be used on the road.

Left: For those who couldn't afford a Jaguar or Ferrari, a whole range of cheap and exciting sports cars were available in the 1950s, such as this Lotus Six.

Below: Switches, knobs, and dials, plus a drilled three-spoke steering wheel in a Chevrolet Corvette V8. What else could the self-respecting sports car buff ask for?

there's no denying that a bucking, roaring Cobra V8 put you close to the action. Or how about the eager, high-revving nature of a tiny Abarth or even tinier Honda S800. Here, rather than just prod and go, the driver had to work in sympathy with a small engine, understand how to get the best from it. If an engine is the key to driving experience, then surely Ferrari's V12s and flat-12s loom large. Their complexity, thoroughbred nature, and glorious noises mean they dominate the cars they power, and whoever's behind the wheel.

Below and right: Not quite a traditional sports car, but not a saloon either. The 1950s two-seat Thunderbird was what Ford called a "personal car," a theme that would resurface with the Mustang ten years later. It outsold the pure sports Corvette in the States anyway, but the American sports car market remained a tiny fraction of the whole.

Left and right: The famous "gullwing" Mercedes 300SL was so nicknamed because of its up and over doors. Fast and high-tech for its time, it pioneered the use of fuel injection on a road car.

We haven't mentioned Porsche yet, in this survey of the different ways in which sports cars highlight the driving experience. Early 911s in particular, with their tail-heavy weight distribution, needed respect or considerable skill (and preferably both) to be driven at the limit on twisty roads. The rear-engine Porsche could snap from understeer to tail-wagging oversteer with very little warning. But for some, mastering these wayward dynamics was what made the 911 a true sports car—that, and its unique flat-six motor.

Porsches have never been cheap, but another type of sports car aimed to offer maximum driving experience at minimum cost. Here, British manufacturers, with later contributions from Italy and Japan, led the way. MG's first post-war Midget, the 1945 TC, sold in big numbers not simply because it was fun to drive, but because it was relatively cheap. A whole string of MGs carried on the tradition—the TD, TF, and 1960s Midget. There were

Above, right, and far right: Ferry, the son of Dr. Porsche, designer of the VW Beetle, was the driving force behind Porsche sports cars. They started out in a small way in war-torn Germany, but within ten years were a major manufacturer. To this day, the rear-engined 911 betrays its VW Beetle roots.

platoons of fiberglass kit cars in the 1950s, '60s, and '70s, cheapish routes to exotic-looking and sports car-feeling experience. Later, when the Midgets and Spitfires had grown old and tired, Fiat reinvigorated the concept with the little mid-engined X1/9. Later still, Mazda's MX-5

introduced the concept of an affordable sports car to the '90s generation.

At the other end of the scale, sheer speed was the thing, the heart of owning a sports car, even if they never got the chance (or had the inclination) to indulge in it. In the '60s, an E-Type promised 150mph, or a Ferrari Superfast nearer 170mph. The mid-engined supercars of the '70s, the Ferarri 512BB and Lamborghini Countach, were supposedly close to 186mph. For the '80s, the F40 and F50 from Maranello were claiming 201 and 202mph respectively. McLaren and Jaguar both claimed 220mph for their ultimate sports cars, the F1 and XJ220.

So, to try and address our original question, what is a sports car, there really is no hard and fast answer to give. Except that a sports car has to look different, more sporting than the equivalent saloon. And it has to put a premium on the driving experience, whatever form that might take. Combine those two elements and you have a sports car.

A Short History

There had been sports cars before the Second World War, lots of them, but they were still chiefly enjoyed by young bloods of the upper and middle classes. The post-war era (1945–70) saw an explosion in the choice available and many sports cars reached true mass production. Some of the most popular reached six- or even

Left and right: No Ferrari badge, but this really is a Ferrari. A prototype of the V6 Dino that took the Italians into a new market for less expensive mid-engined cars.

seven-figure production totals. In Britain, nearly half a million MGBs were built, and over 350,000 Midgets. Mazda made the RX-7 the world's best selling rotary-engined car, with another half-million, while Datsun topped them all, building over a million 240/260Zs. Mass produced, these made sports cars more affordable than ever before, and coupled with a general increase in

Above and right: Mustang, the quintessential muscle car, seen here in one of its most muscle-bound forms, the high revving, rubber burning, tarmac curling Boss 302.

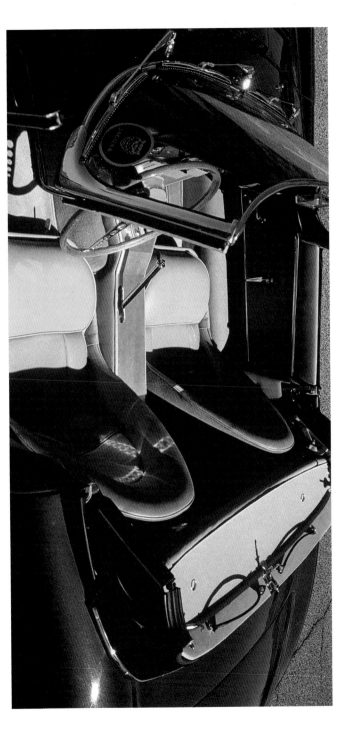

Left and above: Automotive sculpture. Few cars have the beauty and purity of line of the original Jaguar E-Type. Both convertible and fixed-head coupe were simply stunning to look at, the getaway car for a generation.

affluence, it helped to put them within the reach of millions of drivers.

The war had barely ended before MG announced the Midget TC, a small affordable sports car in the same mold as the pre-war TB, and for that matter, the early

Britain was the most prolific sports car maker in the 1950s and '60s—MG, Jaguar, Austin-Healey, Allard, TVR, Triumph, Lotus, Marcos...the list goes on and on. Perhaps one of the unsung heroes was Sunbeam, whose Alpine made a pretty and comfortable alternative to an MGB or Triumph TR3. What it lacked was performance, though once Carroll Shelby had squeezed a Ford V8 under the bonnet to create the Sunbeam Tiger, that cured that.

M-type. This was the first British sports car to find favor in America, and to a nation brought up on Buicks and Cadillacs, the tiny TC must have seemed to come from another planet. Not many of them bought the little MG, but it did start something. Its successor, the TD, sold over 23,000 Stateside, or 80% of the total, setting a pattern for future MGs that would sell faster across the Pond than they ever did in Europe.

While Americans were wondering at the diminutive Brit, Snr. Enzo Ferrari was moving into the sports car business. He had worked for Alfa Romeo before the war, managing a successful racing team, but now set up on his own. The first Ferraris were real sports-racers, designed with competition in mind. In 1946, the first Tipo 125 (the model number referred to the capacity of each cylinder) was a lightweight 1.5 liter V12. That was successively enlarged as the 2.0 liter 166 (1948), the 195 (2.3 liters), 212 (2.5 liters), 340 (with a newly designed 4.0 liter V12), and 375 (4.5 liters).

The Ferraris had started out as they would always be, exotic and expensive pieces of machinery, lovingly assembled, hugely powerful, and charismatic. But they

hardly brought supercar performance to everyman. That fell to Jaguar, whose XK120 of 1948 was a real sports car milestone. Not only was it voluptuously beautiful, and terrifically fast by the standards of the day (the "120" denoted its top speed), but it was cheap. The original XK120 was half the price of anything with comparable performance, and over 12,000 were sold before the XK140 took over in 1954.

In fact, 1948 was a good year for milestones. Porsche commenced production then. Admittedly, they only built four cars, and production built very slowly in a war-torn Germany, but this was the start of a long, long line of individual sports cars. Using the same flat-four engine as the VW Beetle, Ferry Porsche designed a lightweight, aerodynamic car that made the most of its 40bhp. Ferry of course, was son to Dr. Ferdinand Porsche, who had designed the Beetle. Through the 1950s, the Porsche gradually moved away from its Volkswagen roots, with a

1.6 liter/95bhp version of the flat-four by 1955. The four-cam Carrera engine soon followed, and by the time production ended in 1965, over 76,000 had been sold.

Porsches always sold well in America, but the Stateside sports car market was still a tiny fraction of the whole, as some found out to their cost. Briggs Cunningham worked hard to offer an American sports car, using a Chrysler Hemi V8. It had some competition success (though Briggs never quite realized his dream of winning at Le Mans) but didn't sell that well. Even the might of General Motors couldn't crack this market, and the original Chevrolet Corvette of 1953, despite its shapely fiberglass body, good handling, and the option of a V8 power from '55, only sold in tiny numbers. By contrast, Ford sold Thunderbirds by the thousand, as it put luxury features before dynamics.

Meanwhile, back in Britain, the success of MG and Jaguar attracted a whole host of other entrants. Donald Healey's Austin-powered 100 attracted so many orders that his little company couldn't cope. He handed the whole project over to Austin, and the Austin-Healey was born. The 100 had a long and successful life, staying in

Left: What the Italians lacked in numbers, they made up for in sheer *bravura*. This is a Lamborghini Muira, first of the new breed of V12 mid-engined supercars.

production right up to 1967 as the 3000, the six-cylinder "Big Healey." Standard-Triumph announced the TR2 in 1953, the start of another long line of affordable sports cars. An open two-seater in the classic mold, the TR series would include 3, 4, 5, and, in six-cylinder fuel-injected form, the TR6, which died a death in 1975. The TR7 which replaced it was a very different beast. Nor was the small top sports car an exclusively British preserve. The pretty Pininfarina styled Alfa Romeo Duetto offered 1.3, 1.6, or 2.0 liter engines from the late '60s onwards, with fine handling and peppy performance.

At the same time, a young engineer named Colin Chapman was making a name for himself building very lightweight specials, and the Lotus Six from 1952 was a bare, basic sports car that put nimble performance above all other considerations (notably comfort!). That was replaced by the Seven four years later, another long-lived icon in the story of British sports cars was born.

Right: Five short years later, this is what the Muira led to. Lamborghini's outlandish Countach amazed everyone, and kept alive the fierce rivalry with Ferrari.

Left: Ferrari decided to hedge its bets and continued offering front-engined cars alongside the mid-engined type. This 365GTB Daytona carried on the Ferrari tradition of front-engined V12s.

Production was taken over by Caterham in the 1970s, and the company was still building this most basic of all sports cars in 2003.

Lotus made its name with cars whose ultra low weights and superlative handling made up for their small, modestly powered engines. But among the big sports cars of the late 1950s and early '60s, power was the thing. The XK120 had become the 250bhp XK140, then the 265bhp XK150. The stunning E-Type, which replaced the XK, had the same power but was 400lb lighter. And in the Jaguar tradition it had jaw-dropping beauty and a low price tag. Of course, a Ferrari was still the ultimate, with 400bhp claimed for the latest V12, but for Americans, a V8 Corvette was a far cheaper route to high performance, now offering 240bhp. Ford kicked off a new breed in 1964 with the Mustang—the pony car. The Mustang and its many imitators made use of relatively cheap mass produced V8 power until accident rates,

Above: Despite the smaller Dino, Ferrari remained a car for the rich enthusiast. Many people dreamt of owning one, but bought an MG, Alfa Romeo, or Ford.

Left: Porsche stuck with their rear-engined layout for decades, but made it work very well. This four-wheel-drive 959 was the ultimate road-going Porsche of the 1980s.

Right: A simple combination with an explosive result. Squeezing a muscular Ford V8 into the lightweight AC Ace produced the hairy, exciting Cobra. Even today, few road cars can provide quite the same experience.

insurance rates, and emissions and safety legislation all toned down the American muscle car.

Uncertain 'Seventies

But there were alternatives to the conventional front-engine layout. Porsche extended its original concept in 1964 with the six-cylinder 911, a car which in much developed form (only the name and basic layout are unchanged) is still with us today. No one, it has to be said, followed Porsche's rear-engine lead, but Ferrari certainly started something with the mid-engined 250 LM of 1963.

A mid-mounted engine was impractical in some ways, but it also gave theoretically superior weight distribution. From then on, a mid-engined sports car would always

feature in the Ferrari line-up, and its arch-rivals in Italy, notably Maserati and Lamborghini, would follow suit. In fact, from then on, somebody, somewhere in Italy would always be building a mid-engined sports car. Even in the wake of the first oil crisis, Lamborghini launched the striking, cheese-wedge Countach. Claiming over 170mph from its 375bhp 4.0 liter V12, the Countach was unlike anything else, until Ferrari countered with its 512 BB the following year. "BB" stood for "Berlinetta Boxer," denoting Ferrari's first flat-12 engine which powered the latest Maranello car to a claimed 188mph. Ferrari offered slightly less expensive mid-engined cars as well, such as the 308GTB, and notably the Dino, which was actually built by Fiat in an attempt to keep costs down. But it was Fiat who produced the only really affordable mid-engined sports car, in the little X1/9.

At the same time, Triumph replaced the hairy-chested TR6 with the sensible (maybe too sensible) TR7. For the

first time, a Triumph sports car with no convertible option! When the TR7 was on the drawing board many people believed that the American market was about to outlaw open-top cars altogether. Nevertheless, when it was launched, the traditionalists were horrified and despite being a thoroughly modern, comfortable coupe, the latest TR was castigated by the press as well. A convertible option (and the V8 TR8) came later, but perhaps by then it was too late anyway.

In fact, the late '70s were not a happy time for the British sports car. The MG Midget and MGB soldiered on, now hopelessly outdated and encumbered with big plastic bumpers which were demanded by the American market. But MG still sold more cars there than anywhere else. Meanwhile, the Jaguar E-Type had grown fat and heavy, though in its latest V12 form it was just as fast as the original. It was replaced in 1975 by the XJS. Supremely fast and refined, this bigger car that was more of a Grand Tourer than a sports car, though Jaguar sought to address that in the 1980s by producing open-top versions, a 3.6 liter six-cylinder option, and five-speed manual gearbox.

Right: A zesty engine, smart looks, and two seats open to the wind. Alfa Romeo brought all those classic ingredients together in the Spider, and sold it for 27 years.

Porsche also faced a storm of protest when it launched the 924 in 1977. How many conventions could one car break at the same time? The 924 had a front-mounted, water-cooled engine of just four cylinders and 2.0 liters. Its styling came from the anonymous coupe school. And it had originally been designed as an Audi, which showed. However, despite an unpromising start, the 924 led to a whole new line up of Porsches. It was followed by the all-Porsche 928, with a new V8, and which was intended to replace the 911, though never did. The four-cylinder car, meanwhile, acquired a Turbo stablemate and later developed into the 2.5 liter four-cylinder 944. As for the 911, far from being replaced, it too gained a Turbo and kept its ultra-loyal following, outliving the front-engined coupes intended to replace it.

But the 1970s and early '80s were gloomy times for sports car fans. The old school of open cars began to die off, and some companies, such as Aston Martin, went bust altogether. Only Morgan, building a handful of traditional sportsters a week, as it always had done, seemed immune to the gloom. But for everyone else, the effects of two oil crises (there had been another in '79)

and a general tightening up of safety and emissions legislation, threatened to kill off the sports car altogether. Viewed as a selfish, indulgent transport that put out the wrong sort of message, the traditional open two seater seemed out of tune with the times.

It didn't last long though. From 1983 there were signs of a performance revival in America, and if it didn't happen there, then a mass market sports car renaissance was probably impossible. Remember the Mustang? It'd dropped its hot, thirsty V8 options in 1974, as the Mustang II. Customers seemed to appreciate it as the four-cylinder Mustang sold nearly as well as the V8 ever did. But in '83 they were ready to buy into some performance again and Ford launched a V8 Mustang that offered '60s style straight-line performance at a low price.

That was fine for America, but there were signs in the 1980s that sports car were becoming playthings of the rich. As the west recovered from the economic shocks of

the '70s, Porsche moved the 911 ever upmarket. More expensive and high-tech than ever before, it was joined by the four-wheel-drive 959, Porsche's ultimate sports car, which owed much to its racing experience. Ferrari too, seemed to be concentrating on cars for the rich, the Dino being dropped. The Testarossa ("Red head" owing to the color of the cylinder heads) carried on the flat-12 supercar tradition of the BB in 1984. Three years later, the

F40 used twin turbos to boost its V8 up to 471bhp, and a claimed top speed of 201mph. Not wanting to be left out, Jaguar unveiled the limited edition XJ220. The name supposedly reflected the top speed of this twin-turbo V6. Lamborghini claimed 200mph+ for its Diablo.

All these cars were expensive, but all were eclipsed by the McLaren F1. At around half a million pounds (three-quarters of a million dollars) the 600 horsepower F1 was the world's most expensive production car. Extremely high tech and very clever, but then you would expect no less from the designer of countless Formula One racing cars. Alas, just as the bottom dropped out of those red-hot stock markets of the '80s, so a similar thing happened to the hyper-sports cars. Jaguar and McLaren never sold as many cars as they'd hoped.

But in 1989, just when it looked as though the motoring world had polarized into six-figure sports cars for the rich, and dull saloons for everyone else, Mazda came along with the MX-5. This was a masterstroke. Styled in California, it was clearly inspired by the original Lotus Elan of the '60s, slotting neatly into the 1990s trend for "retro"—that is, it somehow looked classic and modern at the same time, but underpinned by thoroughly modern engineering. That was the other thing that ensured the MX-5's huge success, for under the bonnet was a foolproof twin-cam 1.6 liter four-cylinder engine. The whole car was simple, reliable, and well built, as easy to drive as one of Mazda's hatchbacks. What it offered was a taste of the "wind in the hair" '60s motoring, with none of the inconvenience. And people loved it.

So successful was the little Mazda that it virtually kick started a revival of the affordable sports car. Throughout the decade, barely a year went past without some new

Above: Hyper sports cars seemed to proliferate in the 1990s and early 21st century. Like this carbon fiber Pagani Zonda, with 555bhp and a claimed top speed of 220mph.

Right: Four exhaust tailpipes emerging from a 7.3 liter V12. You can't get a much clearer statement of speed than that.

sports car offering. Porsche and Mercedes courted younger, slightly less well-heeled buyers with their Boxster and SLK respectively. Audi announced the compact little TT, Honda the S2000, and Ford brought back the Thunderbird name. Jaguar's XK8 sought to move away from the XJS's GT image, and it later came as a convertible.

But the truly affordable sports cars came from elsewhere. Remember the Fiat X1/9 of the '70s? Well the company came back 20 years later with the more conventional Barchetta, taking Mazda's lead in rounded retro styling. And of course, this revival wouldn't have been complete without an MG. Despite industrial crises and some serious downsizing, MG was still with us, and they launched the mid-engined MGF. Based on mass production mechanical parts, it fulfilled the same role as that original TC of 1945. And that's where we came in, wasn't it?

THE 1940s

A fter six years of war, sports cars were not a priority for most of the world's population. At first, manufacturers offered mild updates of pre-war cars. But within three years of 1945, Ferrari, Porsche, and Jaguar had all launched new models—a foretaste of what was to come.

Left: MG's Midget TC was one of the first post-war sports cars, though it was really little more than a rebadged TB from 1939. Despite that, it was a great success.

Left: It only just qualifies as a sports car of the 1940s, production ended in 1940, but the BMW 328's influence reached well into the post-war world, it was that advanced.

Opposite: The BMW 328 pioneered curvaceous, streamlined bodywork at a time when many sports cars, with separate front wings, betrayed their 1920s origins. It also had independent front suspension (far superior to the more basic set-up on contemporary British sports cars). Not surprisingly, it was fast and handled very well.

BMW 328 Frazer Nash

◻n 1930s Britain, BMWs were imported by Frazer Nash, which was so impressed that it ◻dropped its own line of chain-driven cars in order to concentrate on the more advanced imports. They were badged as "BMW Frazer Nash" (or "Frazer Nash BMW," depending on whom you believe). This 328, with right-hand drive, is one of those. In 1946, one of the streamlined Mille Miglia cars was brought to Britain as part of reparation payments.

Left: A well-stocked dashboard greeted every 328 driver. Not all of these sporting BMWs were raced. The company built over 460 of them, many of which were used as road cars.

Right: A dynamic badge for a dynamic car. Even in road tune, the 328 was a genuine 100mph machine, but the racers packed anything up to 150bhp.

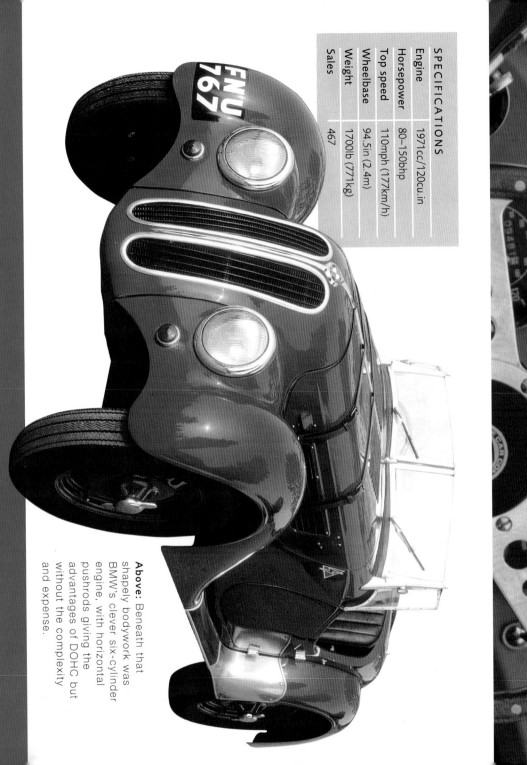

SPECIFICATIONS	
Engine	1971cc/120cu.in
Horsepower	80–150bhp
Top speed	110mph (177km/h)
Wheelbase	94.5in (2.4m)
Weight	1700lb (771kg)
Sales	467

Above: Beneath that shapely bodywork was BMW's clever six-cylinder engine, with horizontal pushrods giving the advantages of DOHC but without the complexity and expense.

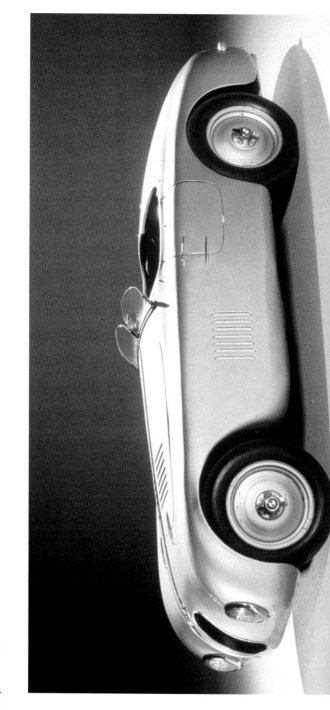

Above: Although remembered as a sports car, the 328 was actually designed as a racer. This is one of five special streamliners which finished first, third, fifth, and sixth in the 1940 Mille Miglia.

Right: The Allard J2—a classic combination. Sydney Allard of North London built sports cars using lightweight British chassis and muscular American V8s, from Ford, Chrysler, or Cadillac. The result was a little crude, but fast and furious.

MG Midget TC

Within months of the end of World War Two, sports cars were rolling off MG's Abingdon (near Oxford, Britain) production lines once again, and the Midget TC led the way. Although little changed from the pre-war TB, it was hugely popular, and 10,000 were sold. Even more significant was that 2000 of those were sent across the Atlantic, paving the way for thousands more British sports cars to Stateside success.

SPECIFICATIONS

Engine	1250cc/76.2cu.in
Horsepower	54 @ 5200rpm
Top speed	73mph (117km/h)
Wheelbase	94in (2400mm)
Weight	1736lb (787kg)
Sales	10,000

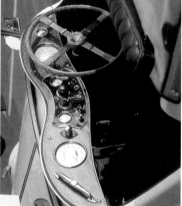

Far left and left: The Midget was never a high performance car, its 1250cc pushrod engine (far left) produced just 54bhp and a top speed of less than 80mph, but the dashboard was authentically sporting.

Right: Top speed hardly mattered for the Midget, it gave an exciting "wind in the hair" ride, and looked the part too. For a world emerging from the shadow of war, that was enough.

Left: After World War Two, Singer reintroduced the perky little roadsters, and this is a typical example. But they had lost the sporting edge of the pre-war Nine and Bantam. In any case, Singer was now more interested in selling saloon cars, and the roadsters were allowed to fade away.

Jaguar SS100

This is the car that launched Jaguar into the big time. For a decade or more, the company had made a good living out of offering swoopy saloons based on cheap, mass production parts. But the SS100, on sale from 1935 to 1941, was a genuine sports car, with a top speed of 100mph and 0–60mph in 10 seconds. That alone made it a seriously fast car for the time, but it was more than that. In the SS/Jaguar tradition, the 100 combined sleek good looks with astonishing value for money. The Jaguar SS100 made high performance affordable for the first time.

Right: Sports car snobs scoffed at the SS100. Its low price and Standard-based engine denied it the breeding of a Bentley or Aston Martin. The "SS" badge was dropped in 1945 for obvious reasons.

Left and below: Under that long bonnet lay a 2.5 liter (later 3.5 liter) Standard straight-six, transformed with overhead valves.

SPECIFICATIONS

Engine	3485cc/213cu.in
Horsepower	125bhp @ 4250rpm
Top speed	100mph (161km/h)
Wheelbase	104in (2640mm)
Weight	2680lb (1215kg)
Sales	n/a

Jaguar XK120

Just as the SS100 caused a sensation in 1935, so did the XK120 13 years later. It had exactly the same three magic points as its predecessor. Stunningly beautiful, the XK looked like nothing else on the road. Incredibly fast, it could top a genuine 120mph when most cars struggled to top 80mph. And being a Jaguar, it also added excellent value for money into the bargain as it was sold for less than half the price of an equivalent sports car of the day. For that buyers could own the fastest production car available.

Right: Some said the XK120 style was inspired by BMW's 328, but the resemblance is slight. Company founder and boss Sir William Lyons was the artist at work.

SPECIFICATIONS

Engine	3442cc/210cu.in
Horsepower	160 @ 5100rpm
Top speed	126mph (203km/h)
Wheelbase	102in (2550mm)
Weight	2929lb (1324kg)
Sales	12,055

Below and right: The XK120 was originally intended as a limited production special, to showcase Jaguar's all-new twin-ohc engine, bound for the MkVII saloon. But the strong public reaction forced the company to rethink and the XK was in production for a total of 13 years.

THE 1950s

The 1950s saw an explosion of sports cars, in choice, price, performance, and technology. New marques, like Porsche, Ferrari, and Jaguar, ran alongside classics from Lancia, Alfa Romeo, and Mercedes. Power increased year on year, but it was the thriving breed of smaller, more affordable sports cars that kept the mass production lines rolling.

Left: The quintessential American sports car, Chevrolet's Corvette was Detroit's answer to the imports coming in from Britain, Italy, and Germany.

Ferrari 166 MM Barchetta

The very first Ferraris of 1946–47 were racing cars, pure and simple. But from November 1948, a range of road-going sports cars was offered, and another legend was born. Those early models were V12s, with the model number referring to the capacity of each cylinder—"125" (125cc per cylinder) was the original 1.5 liter sports racer, and the "166" range, 2.0 liters. All were based around a 60 degree light-alloy V12 unlike anything else available at the time.

SPECIFICATIONS (166 INTER)

Engine	1995cc/122cu.in
Horsepower	108bhp
Top speed	105mph (169km/h)
Wheelbase	96in (2426mm)
Weight	1760lb (800kg)
Sales	36

Right and left: This particular 166 is a Barchetta ("little boat") with bodywork by Touring. It came as an open-top quasi-racer or as a sleek hard top.

Left and above: Like Ferrari, Porsche got into its stride in the 1950s, though as the decade went on, its rear-engined cars owed less and less to their Volkswagen ancestry.

Right: An American oddity. The Kaiser Darrin was an attempt to build a sports car based on a radical design by "Dutch" Darrin. With fiberglass bodywork, sliding doors, and a landau top, it was certainly unusual, but only 435 were ever built.

Porsche 1500 Super America

From the 40bhp 1100cc original of 1948, but Porsche soon moved on. They released a 1300cc option in April 1951, and a 1500 six months after that—1600 and 2.0 liter models would soon follow. All of these models followed the same VW-inspired format of rear-mounted air-cooled flat-four engine, topped by an aerodynamic body. Early Porsches relied on that slippery shape plus light weight, rather than brute power, to create their characteristic high performance on the roads.

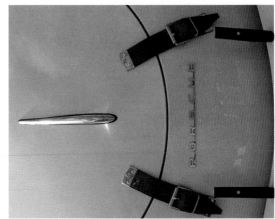

Right: By the late 1950s, America would take nearly 70 per cent of Porsche's production—hence the "Super America" name.

Below: Early Porsche interiors offered functionality and understatement, rather than luxury or the usual sports car-style ostentation.

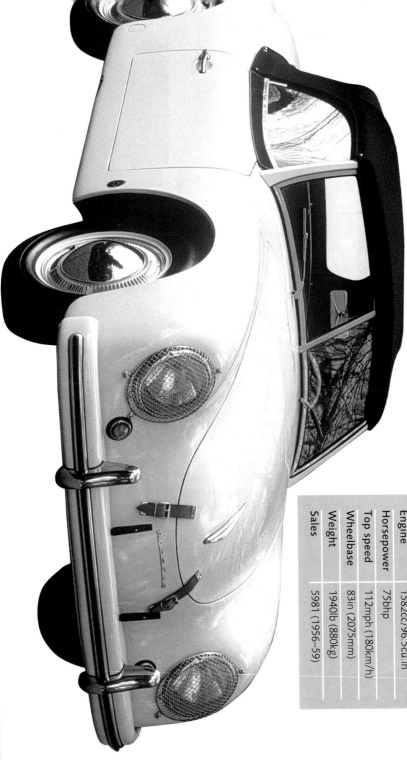

SPECIFICATIONS (1600S)	
Engine	1582cc/96.5cu.in
Horsepower	75bhp
Top speed	112mph (180km/h)
Wheelbase	83in (2075mm)
Weight	1940lb (880kg)
Sales	5981 (1956–59)

Lotus Six 1954

Colin Chapman was 23 when he built the original Lotus. Light in weight, with an aluminum body and independent front suspension, this was powered by a tuned Austin Seven side-valve engine. So successful was the little Lotus in competition that the young engineer decided to go into business, and another famous post-war marque was born. The production Lotus Six was launched in 1953 as a build-it-yourself kit for keen amateurs. They would not be bothered by the lack of doors or other creature comforts, but they would appreciate the wide range of engines available.

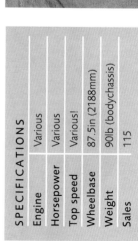

Left, right, and above: The Lotus Six looked almost vintage, but that impression belied the advanced features and original thinking that were lurking just under its simple aluminum panels: a tubular spaceframe and independent front suspension.

SPECIFICATIONS

Engine	Various
Horsepower	Various
Top speed	Various!
Wheelbase	87.5in (2188mm)
Weight	90lb (bodychassis)
Sales	115

Left and above: The C-Type was Jaguar's race winning formula of the early 1950s, which established the company in top-line international racing in general, and the Le Mans 24 hours in particular. Jaguar badly wanted to win this classic French endurance event, but the XK120 sports car was too heavy, and not fast enough, to be competitive. What they needed was a genuine racecar which could make the most of the strong twin-cam XK straight-six.

Right: Aerodynamics was at least part of the answer. The C-Type's basic shape was worked on by Malcolm Sayer, who used his experience in the aircraft industry to produce a supremely slippery design. It showed in a top speed of over 144mph, and a winning Le Mans average of over 100.

Above: C-Types were victorious at Le Mans in 1951 and 1953, though they were plagued by overheating in the intervening year. In that first win, they set a new record average speed of 93.5mph. In 1953, now equipped with disc brakes and triple Weber carburetor, C-Types set a new race-winning average of 105.85mph. Also raced in the famous Mille Miglia, they played a big part in the formative career of rising star Stirling Moss.

Right: This was originally a Healey 100, based on Austin components. But the little Healey company was swamped by demand, so car giant Austin took over the whole project, and Austin-Healey was born. As the six-cylinder "Big Healey" this car would roll off the production lines for nearly a decade and a half.

Left and right: A 1954 facelift for the Jaguar XK120. The new XK140 saw no radical changes, but did standardize the 190bhp version of the XK engine. Heavier bumpers made it less graceful, but the handling was improved and there was more room inside providing greater driving comfort all round.

Below: A famous badge, though the model name no longer referred to top speed—an XK120 would make 120mph, but its successor couldn't manage 140.

Left: The XK140's engine was repositioned compared to that of the 120, to improve handling, and the steering was superior too. There were convenience items like direction indicators, so while the 140 might not look quite as glamorous as the original, it still made a fast, comfortable sports-tourer of its time. Mind you, owners still had to cope with drum brakes all round, which could be alarming in a car as fast and heavy as this.

Right: Like the first XK sports car, this one came as a roadster, drophead convertible, or fixed-head coupe. All of those were two-seaters, and not until the E-Type did Jaguar offer a genuine 2+2 sports car. Six years on from the XK120's sensational debut, the 140 faced some more serious competition, but Jaguar still sold around 9000 of them.

Below: Success in racing means never standing still, and Jaguar followed up the race-winning C-Type, with the even more curvaceous D-Type.

Right: More power and all-round disc brakes allowed the D-Type to win at Le Mans three years running. Brave passengers could be accommodated too!

Jaguar XK SS 1957

With the XK series growing bigger and softer by the year, Jaguar needed another hard-edged sports car. So why not offer a road-going version of the racing D-Type? It would be relatively quick and easy to do, just a matter of adding a windscreen and a couple of other convenience items, no airbags or EPA mileage standards to worry about then. The XKSS, only 16 of which were built in 1957, was the result, though a serious fire at Jaguar's Coventry factory probably prevented it becoming a long-term production car. The more cynical thought it was never intended as such, being no more than a sales ploy to get rid of unsold D-Types. Whatever the reason for its existence, the XKSS—a racer for the road—has achieved cult status.

Right: Despite its practical touches, the XKSS looked every inch the road-racer it was. The bonnet straps, tiny doors, and knock-off wheels betrayed its true racer origins. If Jaguar's softer XK150 was the XK8 of its day, then this was the McLaren F1, promising a true race car experience on the road. And in those days, Britain had no overall speed limit...

SPECIFICATIONS

Engine	3442cc/210cu.in
Horsepower	250bhp
Top speed	144mph (232km/h)
Wheelbase	n/a
Weight	n/a
Sales	16

Above: A neat piece of detailing, combining boot lid handle, Jaguar's head badge, and trim strip on this white XK150 drophead.

Left: Maybe not as sleek as the original, but the XK150 Jaguar was still a stunning looking car in 1957. A higher waistline and one-piece windscreen were the main changes.

Right: Beneath its updated body, the XK150 enjoyed the benefit of all-round Dunlop disc brakes, a real advance on previous XKs. A 3.8 liter engine later replaced the 3.4.

Below: Like every Jaguar sports car before and since, the XK150 shared many parts with equivalent saloons, a major factor that enabled Jaguar to keep the price down.

Below: Before Austin-Healey, there was plain Healey. Donald Healey offered a range of cars powered by Riley's high-cam 2.4 liter four-cylinder engine, and this Silverstone was the most sporting of the lot. It was fast and exciting, though outdated for the day.

Right: Frazer Nash built just 85 cars after World War Two, and this was the most popular. The cigar-shaped Le Mans replica was powered by Bristol's cross-pushrod six-cylinder engine, a development of the pre-war BMW unit.

Left and below: The hand-built Pegaso was the only post-war Spanish sports car produced, with its own V8, five-speed gearbox and De Dion rear suspension. Only around 100 were made in 1951–58.

Right: An American engine, British chassis, and (later) Italian bodywork made the Nash-Healey a truly international car. Built from 1950 to 1954, it combined Healey's existing chassis with the 3.8 liter straight-six Nash engine.

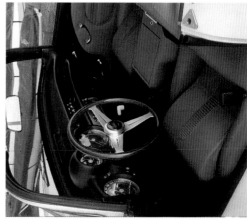

Below: No sports car book would be complete without Morgan. Half a century of steel bodies on ash frames, with the company's own idiosyncratic front suspension, and whatever engine and gearbox happened to be available at the time. This is a Plus 4.

Right: The Cunningham C-3. Briggs Cunningham was a millionaire yacht racer who dreamt of seeing an American car win at Le Mans. His Chrysler V8 powered cars managed third in 1953 and 1954, and a few, with Italian Vignale bodies, were also sold for road use.

Right: Despite its budget price, the TR2 pushed all the right buttons for sports car nuts. It sat them low, increasing the impression of speed, provided bucket seats and a stackload of dials and switches. Couple that with the economy and reliability of Triumph's 1991cc four-cylinder engine, and the TR's success was assured.

Left and above: Back in 1951, Triumph was keen to grab a slice of the lucrative American sports car market, and after a couple of false starts, it did exactly that with the TR2. The first of the long-running TR series was very simple, with a ladder type chassis and straightforward four-cylinder engine, but faster than an MG TF, and well priced too. From the start, it was a winner in both track racing and rallies, which helped to set the seal on its showroom success.

Above: The "6" refers to Austin's 2.6 liter six-cylinder engine, which found its way into the Austin-Healey when the original four-cylinder unit was dropped.

Left: Swoopy full-width styling, punchy performance, and a low price made the Healey 100 an instant hit when it was launched in 1952. So high was demand that the tiny Healey company handed production over to Austin—hence "Austin-Healey." Nearly 15,000 Austin-Healey 100s were built, and over 40,000 of the later 3000, which remained in production until 1967.

Above: The big 100 and 3000 were all very well, but there was still a large market for a small and affordable sports car in 1959. The Sprite was Austin-Healey's answer, delving once more into the parts bins of car giant BMC (of which the Austin-Healey marque was part) to keep costs to a minimum. Not fast, with 43bhp from its 948cc engine, but nearly 50,000 of these "Frog-eye" Sprites found enthusiastic buyers in 1958–61.

Below: The classic Ferrari 375 America. The 375MM (Mille Miglia), on which this car was based, was not a compromise on the original racer it was based on. The racing chasis made a great road car underneath a bodyshell designed by Pininfarina. The ony adjustment was to the engine, which was downrated by little over ten per cent compared to the racing version.

Left, right, and above: Like Jaguar, Porsche, and countless others, Ferrari realized there was a fortune to be made selling sports cars in America. So from the mid 1950s they began producing cars aimed at that market. Larger, more luxurious, and more garish than their European equivalents, they were the 340 America, 375 America, and 410 Superamerica (shown here). All were powered by a large capacity Lampredi-designed V12. In the case of the 410, it was 4.9 liters, and 340bhp at 6000rpm, giving 300bhp/tonne.

Below: In the early 1950s, Chevrolet had a careful eye on the success of Jaguar, MG, and Ferrari in America, and decided to build its own sports car. The 1953 Corvette certainly caused quite a stir.

Right: The Corvette used a fiberglass bodyshell, relatively quick and easy to restyle, so the '54 was given more character, plus that vital ingredient of a V8 option over the lackluster Blue Streak six.

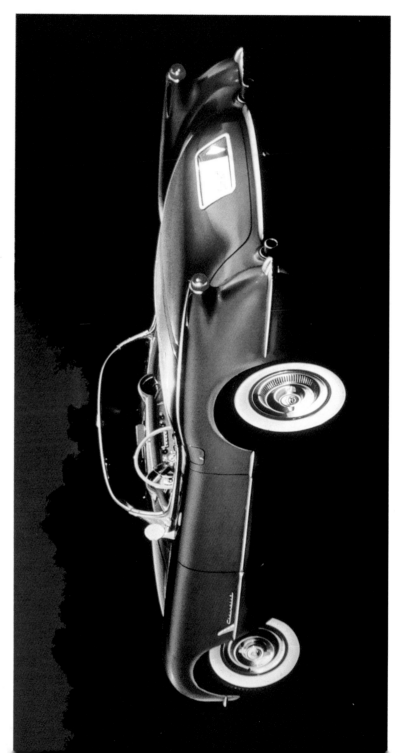

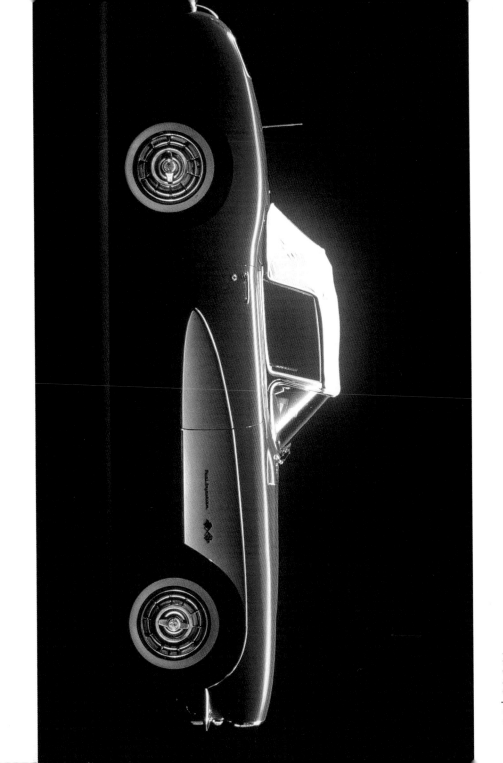

Chevrolet Corvette V8

Chevrolet's original Corvette was a flop. On one hand, it was too expensive for young MG buyers; on the other, it lacked the creature comforts that appealed to the mass of American drivers. But the real gap in its armor was performance, or rather the lack of it. Even though tuned, the aged Blue Streak six couldn't keep up with many V8 sedans. Fortunately, Chevrolet had the answer ready.

Below left: An authentically sporting steering wheel, part of the showroom appeal that helped to sell the Corvette to the American public.

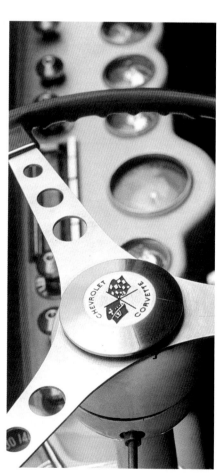

Below: Restyling the Corvette's fiberglass body was relatively quick and cheap, so this new shape soon followed the original. Twin headlights and an optional hard top came later.

SPECIFICATIONS (1962 V8)

Engine	5359cc (327cu in)
Horsepower	360bhp
Acceleration	0–60: 5.9 secs
Transmission	3 or 4-speed manual
Weight	n/a
Sales (all '62)	14,531

Above and left: A 255hp V8 option transformed the Corvette's performance, as did a three-speed manual transmission. In the early '60s, the top 327 V8 with fuel injection offered 360hp.

Right: Part of the first Corvette facelift was a more luxurious interior with practical touches like wind-up windows. It all helped, but the two-seat Chevrolet never matched the success of Ford's Thunderbird.

Left: Very rare, the Aston Martin DB4 GT Zagato was a special edition of a limited production car. The basic DB4 (launched in 1959) spawned the lighter, more sporting DB4 GT, which was tested by *Autocar* at over 150mph. Only 74 of the short wheelbase GTs were built, but this Zagato, with bodywork by the famous Italian coach house, was rarer still, and just 19 cars were ever completed.

Right: This was Aston Martin's answer for Jaguar's C-Type—the DB3S. The first DB3 was a designed as a racer, but was too slow and under-developed to frighten Jaguar. But the DB3S which followed in 1953 was something else again. Smaller, lighter, and more powerful, it was truly competitive, winning five major races in its debut year (though it had a disastrous Le Mans). The company sold 20 to keen privateer racers, who scored many more wins, and by 1956 the DB3S was producing 230bhp.

Aston Martin DB2/4 Mark III

As much a 2+2 Grand Tourismo as a pure sports car, the Aston Martin DB2/4 grew out of the original DB2 of 1950. It made use of the fine Lagonda DOHC six-cylinder engine (both Aston Martin and Lagonda had been taken over by David Brown) which gave smooth performance, especially in uprated Vantage form. With its 2+2 seating and hatchback rear end, this Aston was a truly practical sports car.

Below far left: Early DB2/4s used the same 2580cc engine as the DB2, with 105 or 120bhp. Later this was enlarged to 2922cc, with up to 162bhp from the final MK IIIB DB2/4.

Left and right: There's no denying that the early Astons were handsome cars. Some said they were the rich man's Jaguar, or maybe the not-quite-so-rich man's Bristol.

SPECIFICATIONS

Engine	2922cc/178cu.in
Horsepower	162bhp
Top speed	120mph (193km/h)
Wheelbase	n/a
Weight	n/a
Sales	n/a

Above: A glorious failure from BMW. The svelte 507, launched in 1956, was a thing of beauty. Fast too, thanks to its own 3.2 liter aluminum V8, with a top speed of up to 140mph. Alas, it was three times the price of a Corvette, and less than 300 were sold.

Right: Far more down to earth (and not to mention cheaper) was the MGA, which appeared in 1955 to replace the ageing TF. Fun and affordable, over 100,000 MGAs were sold in a seven-year production run, over 80 per cent of them in America.

Left and below: The last of a line. This car was made history by the MGA. The TF was the last of the long-running T-series, and its roots stretched back to the first TA Midget of 1935. Unveiled in 1953, it was a mild restyle of the TD, with more flowing front wings, a raked-back radiator and faired-in headlamps. MG hoped this would hold the fort until the all-new MGA came on stream two years later.

Above and left: By the mid-1950s, with a whole range of younger competitors tempting buyers, the TF Midget was very much a car for traditionalists. But for the diehards, even the TF wasn't quite traditional enough to be a real MG, though they had said exactly the same of the 1935 TA. The MGA, in its turn, was castigated as too soft and comfy to be a real sports car, as was the later MGB. With 100 per cent rose-tinted vision, all of these were later seen as classic sports cars. *Plus ca change...*

Left and below: Was the Bristol a true sports car? The company preferred the term "businessman's express," especially when applied to the short wheelbase 404. All early Bristols were powered by a development of BMW's pre-war cross-pushrod six-cylinder engine. They were highly aerodynamic (Bristol's main business was aircraft), very well made, expensive, and exclusive. The company later abandoned its BMW-derived six in favor of a Chrysler V8.

Right: The elegant sophistication of the AC Aceca—hard to believe that this led directly to the rude and hairy AC Cobra. Both had their origins in the AC Ace of 1953. The Aceca coupe (mechanically identical to the Ace, with a choice of AC, Bristol, or Ford sixes) arrived the following year. Like the Ace, it used independent transverse-leaf suspension all round. In a seven-year run, only 1057 Aces and Acecas were built.

Left: A British sports car with a difference. The Jowett Jupiter was powered by a 1486cc flat-four engine, shared with the Javelin saloon, plus an aluminum bodyshell. Alas, Jowett was too small to compete with the big boys, and ceased production in 1954. Only 1000 Jupiters were built.

Above: Italian beauty. The Lancia Aurelia boasted the first mass produced V6 engine, plus all-round independent suspension and, for near-perfect weight distribution, a rear-mounted transaxle. This Spider, with styling by Pininfarina, was the sports car of the range.

Below: The 1954 Thunderbird was promoted by Ford as a "personal car" rather than a true sports car. Ten years later it would claim the same for the first Mustang.

Right: With V8 power from the start, luxury features, and a comfortable ride, the Thunderbird was a success—54,000 were sold in 1955–57. That wasn't enough for Detroit though, so a new four-seat T-bird followed in '58.

Mercedes 300 SL Gullwing Coupe

Fuel injection, a spaceframe chassis, and a top speed of over 160mph. The Mercedes 300SL sounds like a sports car of the 1980s, even the '90s. Yet it was launched a half-century ago, the first car to use a multi-tube spaceframe, and one of the first road cars to offer fuel injection. It was developed from the sports-racing 300SL, which won at its Le Mans debut in 1952. Complex, and expensive to make, the Gullwing was later joined by a convertible with conventional doors.

SPECIFICATIONS

Engine	2996cc/183cu.in
Horsepower	215bhp @ 5,800rpm
Top speed	165mph (299km/h)
Wheelbase	95in (2400mm)
Weight	3,000lb (1,364kg)
Sales	3,250

Above and left: There are no doubts, this is a sports car. The gullwing doors weren't just a marketing ploy. Mercedes was reluctant to compromise that spaceframe chassis with the big openings needed by conventional doors.

Right: In its time, this was the fastest car on the market, with 165mph claimed on the right gearing. But the flexible fuel injected six would also pull from 15mph in top gear.

Right: Sometimes simple is best. The original Lotus Seven (just like all its descendants) was little more than a few alloy panels bolted to a lightweight spaceframe, plus an engine and suspension. Sold in kit form, it avoided some sales tax, thus offering almost racecar handling for very little money. A winning formula, and nearly half a century later, the Seven is still in production.

Left: Ferrari in miniature? A successful tuning parts business allowed Carlo Abarth to concentrate on building a series of pretty coupes through the 1950s and '60s. Most were based on Fiat parts and all extracted high performance from tiny engines.

Below left and right: Big performance from small engines was Abarth's trademark. His first 110cc coupe of 1950 could top 110mph, and an official association with Fiat began in 1956 with a tuned version of the little 600 saloon. Fiat later took over the company.

THE 1960s

3

Was this a golden age for sports cars? Safety and emissions legislation had had to take hold, incomes were rising, and high-octane fuel was relatively cheap. Sports cars had enjoyed a decade and a half's development since World War Two. They were fun, fast, and of their time.

Left: A concept rooted in the 1950s, but the Lotus Seven continued to sell well through the '60s—there would always be a market for basic, thrilling cars like this.

PROFILE

Left and above: Carroll Shelby had the idea of shoehorning a big Ford V8 into the little AC Ace. The legend outweighed the car, for the Cobra never sold in big numbers, but it remains one of the hairiest sports cars of all time.

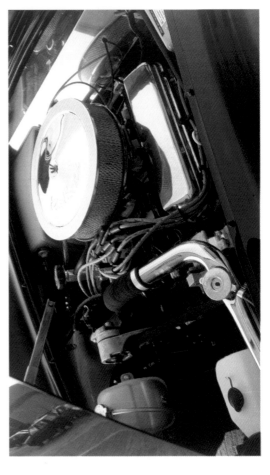

AC Cobra

Nothing personifies the '60s more (in car terms) than the AC Cobra. Loud, proud, and dangerous, it combined American V8 muscle with a light weight British sports car, and the result was stunningly fast, but rather inclined to bite back!

Below: This isn't a genuine '60s Cobra at all, but an Autokraft replica. The Cobra ceased production in 1968, but its reputation was such that countless replicas have been offered since.

SPECIFICATIONS (65 427)	
Engine	6998cc/427cu.in
Horsepower	425bhp @ 6,000rpm
Top speed	165mph (266km/h)
Wheelbase	90in (2290mm)
Weight	2282lb (1035kg)
Sales	1011 (all types)

Below: Alpine was the name for Sunbeam's attractive two-seater of the early '60s, designed by the Rootes Group to counter MG and Austin-Healey. Power came from a 1725cc four-cylinder engine.

Opposite: It looked nice enough, but the Alpine was starting to lag as the decade went on. So Rootes asked Carroll Shelby to give it the Cobra treatment. The 4.2 liter V8 Sunbeam Tiger was the result.

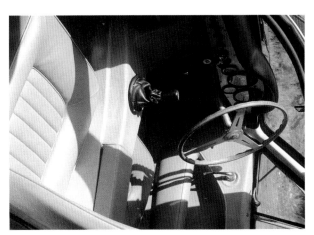

Left: In the 1960s, Aston Martins became fast, heavy grand tourers, the DB5 and DB6 having seating for four, and the same 4.0 liter six-cylinder engine as the DB4. An all-new 5.3 liter V8 in late 1969 would be the basis of a new generation of Astons, but for now, the wire-wheeled sixes were immortalized as 007 James Bond's personal transport.

Left: It looks plush from this angle, but the Elite was noisy at speed and the windows wouldn't even wind down. But on hot days though they could be taken out altogether!

Below: You could still buy a Lotus Elite in 1961, but not for long. Too expensive to sell in big numbers, it was eventually dropped to make way for the Elan.

Left: The Austin-Healey 3000, the final incarnation of the "Big Healey" now with the 2912cc version of BMC's six-cylinder pushrod engine. The Big Healeys did well in long distance rallies.

Below: The world was changing around the Big Healey, but it remained a traditional sports car for the committed. Only the advent of new safety legislation in late '60s America (its chief market) marked the end.

Below: Compare this Aston Martin DB6 with the DB5 on page 130. The differences are subtle, but the rear end was cleaned up, as the 5's small fins disappeared. Aston itself nearly disappeared in the years that followed.

Right: America was captivated by Chevrolet's new Corvette, the Sting Ray, in 1962. So much so, that 20,000 were sold in '63 alone, and buyers were forced to wait two months to take delivery.

Above: In 1968, Chevrolet dropped the original Sting Ray in favor of this. Some thought it a retrograde step, but in its turn, the '68 Corvette came to be seen as a classic too. This is the top-spec L88 coupe, with a 427 V8 of 425bhp.

Right: Pontiac Firebird, another GM response to the success of the Ford Mustang. It later became the more celebrated Trans Am, but it started production as little more than a restyled Chevrolet Camaro, though with Pontiac's own sixes and V8s.

Above, right, and far right: Hard to believe that these two cars (the Daimler Dart above and the Datsun 240Z opposite) hail from the same decade, but they do. The difference lies in the concept. Daimler's sports car, though launched in 1959, was firmly 1950s in concept—the only exception to this was its small (2.5 liter) free-revving V8 in place of a traditional straight four or six. The Datsun on the other hand, was launched in 1969 with its eyes looking forwards to the '70s. Designed to meet all the latest safety and emissions legislation, it could top 120mph yet was as convenient and reliable as a Japanese family car. It led to a long line of Z-series Datsun/Nissans, but the Dart was Daimler's last sports car.

Below: The De Tomaso Mangusta, a marriage between Italian supercar style and American V8 muscle. Alejandro de Tomaso realized that complex Italian engineering (such as Ferrari's V12) were just too much trouble for most American drivers. So he designed an authentic Italian supercar around Ford's reliable V8. It wasn't quite a marriage made in heaven, but it certainly lasted.

Above: An Elva Courier at speed. Elva was one of the many British kit car manufacturers that thrived in the '60s. They supplied their own fiberglass bodies to fit mass production mechanical parts.

Right: This Facel Vega was the nearest thing to a French-made GT after World War Two. It used a De Soto V8, though the smaller, more sporting Facellia used the company's own 1.6 liter twin cam four. Neither was built in large numbers.

Above and right: Everyone remembers the GTO, but cars like the Superfast 500 were Ferrari's bread and butter. That's if you can call a 400bhp V12 capable of over 170mph a bread and butter car.

Left: Ferrari 250 GTO. The letters stood for "Gran Turismo Omologato" but don't be fooled by the "GT" part—this was no Grand Tourer, but a sports-racer, and Ferrari had to build 100 of them for homologation. The six-carburetor 300bhp V12 revved to 8400rpm.

Ferrari Dino 206

Y ou are looking at the closest thing yet to a budget Ferrari. This is the prototype Dino V6 from 1966, a car which Ferrari hoped would take the company into a bigger market for smaller, cheaper sports cars. To cut costs, the engine was built by Fiat (though designed by Ferrari) and there was a Fiat, badged Dino as well. In full production by 1968 as the Dino 206, it became the 2.4 liter 246 the following year.

Above and left: Placing the 2.0 liter V6 amidships gave the little Dino good weight balance and fine handling. Small and lightweight, the Dino was in many ways a return to the early Ferrari trademarks. The four-cam V6 came in 160bhp (Fiat) and 180bhp (Ferrari) guises. Having it built by Fiat not only brought the price down, but it was also relatively easy for Fiat to assemble the 500 engines needed for homologation in Formula 2 racing.

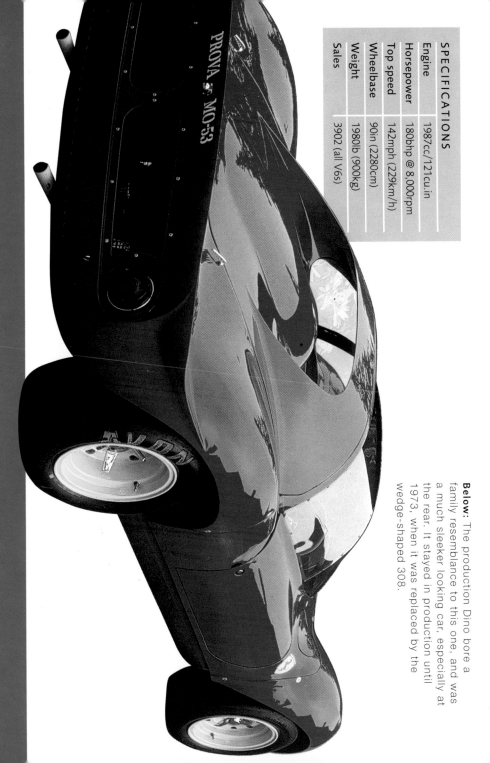

PROVA MO-53

SPECIFICATIONS

Engine	1987cc/121cu.in
Horsepower	180bhp @ 8,000rpm
Top speed	142mph (229km/h)
Wheelbase	90in (2280cm)
Weight	1980lb (900kg)
Sales	3902 (all V6s)

Below: The production Dino bore a family resemblance to this one, and was a much sleeker looking car, especially at the rear. It stayed in production until 1973, when it was replaced by the wedge-shaped 308.

Below: Ferrari 250GT Lusso, or "luxury racer" to some. All of these were designed and built by Pininfarina, but the engine was pure Ferrari, a 3.0 liter V12 of 240 or 250bhp, depending on tune.

Far right: Ford's Mustang pioneered the pony car concept, using tried and trusted components in a practical four-seater with sports car looks. This was Ford's fastest-selling car since the Model T.

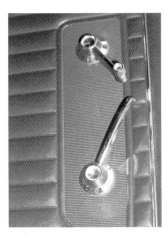

Above and below: Details counted on the Mustang. Above all, this was a car which needed to impress customers both in the showroom, on the driveway, and outside the shops. And it did.

Ford Mustang Shelby GT 500

Sporty looks at a low price, plus a long, long option list to personalize your new car—these were the reasons for the Mustang's success. Ford sold over 400,000 in the first full year. Carroll Shelby took the car racing, and began tuning Mustangs at his California base. These personified the muscle car generation. Hertz even bought a few hundred Shelby Mustangs to hire out to weekend racers!

Below left and right: The early Shelby Mustangs really were racers for the road. They came complete with roll bar, rock-hard suspension, and a stripped-out interior. But within a couple of years they had been toned down and civilized.

Right: Carroll Shelby fitted a big-block V8 to the Mustang before Ford did itself. The result was a tire smoking muscle car with astonishing straight line performance.

SPECIFICATIONS

Engine	7014cc/428cu.in
Horsepower	360bhp
Top speed	120mph (190km/h) est
Wheelbase	108in (2740mm)
Weight	3370lb (1532kg)
Sales	7300 (approx)

Above and left: The Mustang started out as a compact car (that's compact by American standards) but it soon put on fat. This is the '69 version—bigger, heavier, and more powerful than the original.

Right: Mustangs are associated with powerful V8s, but the basic six-cylinder option sold well right through the 1960s. The 1966 Sprint package on this six-cylinder convertible added some snazzier look-at-me parts, while still retaining the six's fuel economy.

Jaguar XKE 1963

S100, XK120, E-Type. The long line of fast, good looking, and value for money Jaguar sports cars continued into the '60s with the E-Type, which in America was known as the XKE. Just like its predecessors, the latest "Jag" was fast (150mph was possible, just) and astonishingly good value. And of course, it was a real stunner.

Nothing looked quite like an E-Type, the ultimate '60s "getaway car."

Left and below: The XK engine's finest hour? In original E-Type form, the 3.8 liter gave 265bhp with triple SU carburetors. A more torquey 4.2 liter followed in 1964. Wire wheels were a popular option.

Right: Malcolm Sayer, the stylist/aerodynamicist who penned the C- and D-Types, was given a free hand with the E. Rarely have aerodynamics and good looks gone so well together.

SPECIFICATIONS ('63)

Engine	3781cc/231cu.in
Horsepower	265bhp
Top speed	150mph (242km/h)
Wheelbase	96in (2350mm)
Weight (V12)	3230lb (1453kg)
Sales	72,520 (all types)

Left: Three wipers were needed to clear the E-Type's low, wide windscreen. Underneath one of the longest bonnets in the business was a monocoque body/chassis bolted to a tubular steel front frame—the XK150's separate chassis had gone. As for the 150mph top speed, that was only just possible if you specified the optional Dunlop racing tires. But whatever tires it wore, the original E-Type was a very quick car indeed.

Right: Many E-types were sold as convertibles. It was one of the fastest open-top cars in the world, and if the pretty fastback had any faults, they included a cramped interior and poor ventilation. Both cars suffered from a non-syncromesh first gear and indifferent dynamo-powered electrics. An all-syncromesh gearbox and alternator electrics soon cured that, while the 2+2 coupe from 1966 was a little roomier.

Right: From this angle, the slightly later 4.2 liter E-Type looks just like the original, but much later V12 cars were altogether more bulbous and less attractive. But for speed nuts, the V12 did restore performance to the original levels, while complying with 1970s emissions legislation.

Far right: Italian coachwork plus American V8 meant Iso Grifo as well as De Tomaso. Renzo Rivolta was a successful Italian industrialist who launched the Chevrolet powered Rivolta in 1962. This four-seat coupe was more Grand Tourer than sports car, and offered a Chevy auto transmission or ZF four-speed manual. The Grifo shown here was introduced the following year, with an all new body clothing the same mechanical parts. All except the last few used Chevrolet V8s, culminating in the 7.5 liter "Can Am" V8 of nearly 400bhp. Production ceased in 1975 when Iso itself ceased to exist.

Left: In the early 21st century, four-wheel-drive cars are common and anti-lock brakes almost compulsory, but back in 1966 the Jensen Interceptor FF was the only car to offer either of these, let alone both. With a big Chrysler V8 engine, the FF was fast, complex, and expensive. It was ahead of its time too, as it would be another 20 years before four-wheel-drive and ABS became readily available options. In the late '60s, most buyers went for the cheaper two-wheel-drive Jensen.

Right: Before the Touring-designed Interceptor, there was the CV-8. The Jensen brothers were fitting big American V8s to their cars in the 1930s, so this was nothing new. The fiberglass CV-8 was a true grand tourer. Not exactly beautiful, but it could seat four in reasonable comfort, then whisk them and their luggage across countries at high speed.

Porsche 356B

The year of 1964 marked Porsche's coming of age. Not only was it selling more cars than ever before, it sold more in '64 than in the previous ten years combined, but it was the first full year of production for the 911. And the last full year for the 356, Porsche's first car, which had kicked off production back in 1948. Since then, it had seen many changes, it had grown in size from a 40bhp 1100 to a 90bhp 1600, and finally, a 2.0 liter. The 356 had established Porsche as a respected manufacturer.

Below left: The 356B, produced from 1959 onwards, was really the ultimate 356, with a 90bhp version of the air-cooled flat-four, improved syncromesh and finned aluminum brake drums (though not discs yet).

Below: What didn't change (at least in the basic outline) was the 356's beetle-backed shape, so familiar to a couple of generations of Porsche lovers; it was designed by Austrian Irwin Kommeda.

SPECIFICATIONS

Engine	1582c/97cu.in
Horsepower	90bhp @ 5500rpm
Top speed	110mph (177km/h)
Wheelbase	83in (2100mm)
Weight	1985lb (900kg)
Sales	30,963 (356B only)

Porsche 911 Coupe

[]t might look similar to the 356, but the Porsche 911 was completely new. All it shared with the old car was the badge, basic mechanical layout, and a family resemblance. It would be the backbone of Porsche's range for 40 years, and you can't be much more of a backbone than that.

SPECIFICATIONS

Engine	1991cc/121cu.in
Horsepower	130bhp
Top speed	130mph (209km/h)
Transmission	5-speed
Weight	2380lb (1080kg)
Sales	10,723 (1964–67)

Left and right: Underneath that familiar shape, the 356's air-cooled four was dropped in favor of a 2.0 liter six, which in 911S form offered 160bhp, enough for over 130mph. Engine sizes and power figures crept up over the decades, though the 911 stuck with that flat-six layout. But even the 1970s Porsche Turbo, with twice the power of the original 911, kept that family look.

Below: The '60s saw Maserati transform from a specialized maker of racecars to one of the Italian supercar standards. This beautiful Mistrale Spyder was styled by Frua and powered by a fuel-injected version of Maserati's own 3.7 liter straight six.

Right: Morgan kept up to date, not with its hand beaten bodywork and separate chassis, but with contemporary engines. The '60s saw a choice of tuneable Ford four-cylinder units, from 997cc to 1598cc. This is the 4/4.

Below: Triumph's GT6 was something of a miniature E-Type for those who couldn't afford the real thing. It used a shapely fastback conversion on the little Spitfire along with Triumph's smooth 2.0 liter six.

Opposite: The four-cylinder TR4A looked like a more traditional British sports car, but underneath had all independent coil spring suspension and, with the 1967 TR5, a fuel-injected 2.5 liter six.

Right: MG's most popular car ever was the MGB, though the bonnet bulge gives this one away as an MGC, using BMC's 2.9 liter six-cylinder engine. The four-cylinder B was far more successful, thanks in part to the reliable 1798cc engine and the choice of two-seat open top and 2+2 fastback GT versions. It was comfortable, with plenty of room for two people and their luggage. And its success cannot be overstated. Over half a million MGBs were sold over an 18-year production run, making it the best selling single-model sports car of all time.

Above: Few people now associate Volvo with sports cars, but the P1800 coupe was popular in the '60s, and achieved fame as Roger Moore's transport in "The Saint" TV series. This is a later P1800 Estate.

Right: Beneath the customized surface is a Studebaker Hawk GT, Studebaker's last throw of the dice before ending car production in 1966. The ageing Hawk V8 was revamped in record time, but it wasn't enough to save Studebaker.

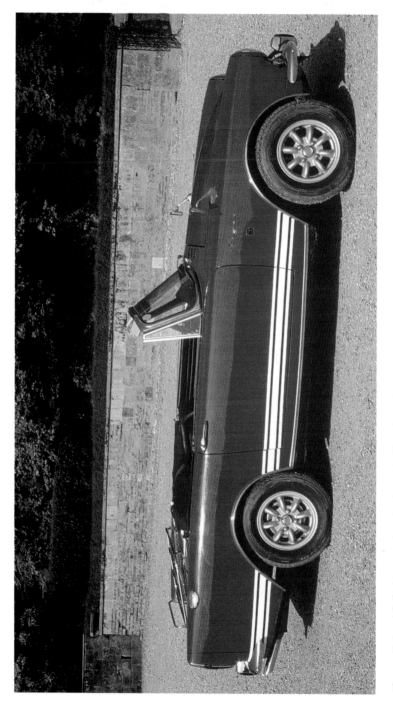

Above: If the AC Cobra was too basic and all-action, then this Sunbeam Tiger promised to be a more civilized version of the same thing. It was also much cheaper. Carroll Shelby shoehorned a 4.2 liter Ford V8 under the Sunbeam Alpine's bonnet, but the production cars were made in Britain.

Right: It was a tight fit, but it worked, offering twice the power (164bhp) of the four-cylinder Alpine, and with the later 4.7 liter V8, 125mph performance. Over 7000 Tigers were sold, but Chrysler's takeover of Sunbeam quickly killed off this Ford-engined car.

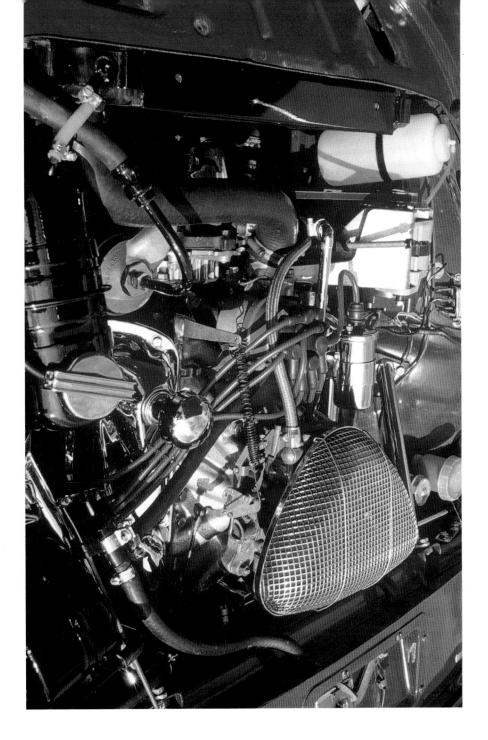

Below: The Ginetta G4 was one of the better British kit cars, featuring a spaceframe chassis and fiberglass body, with or without hardtop. It was Ginetta's most successful car of the '60s, offering a choice of Ford engines spanning 1200, 1340, or 1498cc. Many G4s proved successful in competition—the space frame chassis gave fine handling, and the little car's low weight (around 1120lb) ensured good performance.

Above and right: Tractor manufacturer Ferruccio Lamborghini went into the sports car business in 1963 after (so the story goes) a snub from Enzo Ferrari. And this was the result, the front-engined 350GT, a V12 Grand Tourer aimed directly at the equivalent Ferrari. Unusually, Lamborghini made almost every part in-house, including the gearbox. The 350 was later uprated as the 400GT 2+2, with the V12 enlarged to 3.9 liters and 320bhp.

Left and above: For 1960, Lotus unveiled the Series II Seven, with weather protection standard and 13-inch wheels allowing a wider choice of tires. The biggest news was the availability of Ford's revvy little 997cc engine. And best of all the new Seven was cheaper than the old one.

Right: To be a credible Italian supercar manufacturer, Lamborghini had to offer a mid-engined sports car, and this was it, the P400 Muira, sporting the same 3.9 liter V12 as the front-engined GT.

Right: Matra, a French aeronautical engineering firm, unveiled its first sports car in 1965. The MS530 looked good, and was powered by Ford's compact 1.5 liter V4 engine, but a limited dealer network held back sales.

Below: Purposeful sports car interior for the MS530, but Matra didn't have the resources to go it alone, so decided to team up with an existing car manufacturer.

Right: Simca was the French manufacturer that Matra joined with in 1969, which really meant the end of the pretty, but Ford powered, MS530. In the meantime, Matra had been busy building engines for Formula One racing, and in 1973 launched the Simca-based Bagheera, a 1.4 liter mid-engined fiberglass bodied sports car. In 1980 that was replaced by the steel bodied Murena, and later still Matra developed the Espace people carrier for Renault.

Lotus Elan Plus 2

Lotus needed a cheaper, more affordable sports car to replace the expensive Elite, and the 1963 Elan, with its steel backbone chassis and Ford-based twin-cam engine, did just that. It was small, light and distinctive, and despite a less purist specification than the Elite, handled like a dream. A few years later, with Lotus customers grown a little older, often with young families, a four-seat Elan was the next step.

Left and right: This was it, the Elan Plus 2 shared most of its mechanical parts with the two-seater, but looked quite different, thanks to an extra 12 inches of wheelbase. The prototype looked too long and narrow, so Colin Chapman added seven inches to the width as well. The wedge-like front end gave a drag coefficient of just 0.30— stunningly efficient for the time.

SPECIFICATIONS

Engine	1558cc/95cu.in
Horsepower	118bhp
Top speed	122mph (196km/h)
Wheelbase	96in (2400mm)
Weight	1848lb (840kg)
Sales	4600 approx

THE 1970s

4

Two oil crises, ever tightening emissions and safety legislation, unemployment and inflation. The 1970s were not a happy time for the sports car—some said the traditional open-top two-seater would soon disappear altogether. That didn't happen, but it certainly lay dormant for a few years.

Left: Related to the 1960s Lamborghini Miura, the dramatic Countach of 1974 looked very different. With a mid-mounted V12, it claimed a top speed of around 180mph.

Morgan Plus 8

For longer than anyone could remember, Morgan had lagged behind in the performance race. That all changed with the Plus 8. In talks with Rover about a takeover (which didn't happen) Peter Morgan asked if he could try fitting Rover's compact, powerful 3.5 liter V8 to the four-cylinder Plus 4. It worked, and the Plus 8 was born, instantly catapulting Morgan into the league of fast cars.

SPECIFICATIONS

Engine	3528cc/215cu.in
Horsepower	155bhp
Top speed	120mph (193km/h)
Wheelbase	98in (2450mm)
Transmission	4/5-speed manual
Sales	n/a

Left and right: Perhaps the most remarkable thing about the Plus 8 was how little it was changed from the Plus 4. A slightly longer wheelbase and wider track, and that was it. Weighing little, it would accelerate faster than an E-Type Jaguar, with the burbling exhaust note providing a delightful backdrop. The suspension was still hard and uncompromized, but Morgan gradually updated the Plus 8 over the years with a five-speed gearbox and fuel injection.

Opposite: Triumph's Stag was a brave attempt to build a four-seat GT, with its own 3.0 liter V8 and a hardtop or soft top. Poor reliability let it down.

Below: The odd little three-wheel Bond Bug (this is a later four-wheel conversion) was more fun car than sports car, with unique cheese-wedge looks.

Jaguar E-Type V12

The E-Type's fast-car status had been gradually eroded by emissions controls on the ageing XK engine. The only answer was an all-new unit, and Jaguar responded with a super-smooth overhead cam V12—top speed-wise, Jaguar was back in performance contention.

SPECIFICATIONS

Engine	5343cc/326.5cu.in
Horsepower	272bhp @ 5850rpm
Top speed	150mph (241km/h)
Wheelbase	105in (2625mm)
Weight	3230lb (1453kg)
Sales	15,290

Left: In development since 1968, the 5.3 liter V12 offered 272bhp, and would remain part of the Jaguar range for years to come. Fuel injection soon replaced the four carburetors, but it always drank fuel at an alarming, even amoral, rate.

Below: This was a very different E-Type to that sleek original. The Series III V12 had put on weight, and had become more of a Grand Tourer than a true sports car.

Right: The V12's origins lay in Jaguar's DOHC XJ13 racer of 1966, but proved superbly refined on the road.

Left and above: This car took Jaguar into the exclusive club of manufacturers offering a V12 in the 1970s. The engine was designed by Jaguar engineer Claude Bailey, simplified from the XJ13 with a single overhead cam per bank of cylinders. It was still a complex engine, yet weighed only 65lb more than the XK six, thanks to aluminum cylinder heads. In later fuel injected form, it produced 300bhp.

Below: Jaguar's 1975 replacement for the E-Type was the XJS, seen here in customized form. With the 5.3 liter V12 standard (now with fuel injection) it was even more of a Grand Tourer, larger and heavier than the E-Type, and with four seats. Most were ordered with automatic transmission, though Jaguar later sought to boost its sporting credentials by fitting the new AJ6 engine and a five-speed gearbox.

Below: Just as the Jaguar E-Type put on middle-aged spread in the early 1970s, so did Ford's Mustang. Lee Iacocca, the man behind the original '64 Mustang, described a later version as "a fat pig."

Right: Some things hadn't changed though. The Mustang still came in convertible or coupe form, and there was a wide range of engines, transmissions, and other options to choose from.

Mercedes 280SL

Mercedes, famous for the fire-breathing 300 Gullwing, also offered the mild-mannered SL two-seaters, a long line that stretched back to the 190SL of 1955. Some said they were too soft to be real sports cars, but the 280SL (from 1968) had 120mph performance, and the 1970s would see ever faster and more powerful SLs, culminating in the 5.0 liter 500SL V8, which was built up to 1989.

Right: This 280 was the first SL ("Sports Light") Mercedes to offer serious performance, thanks to its 2.8 liter overhead cam six-cylinder engine. Most still came with automatic transmission, but all had a detachable hard top that would not leak.

Left: The SL's functional saloon origins showed in its relatively stark dashboard, though later cars would be more plush. Its real strength was in comfort, solidity, and convenience, and in 280 form, performance as well.

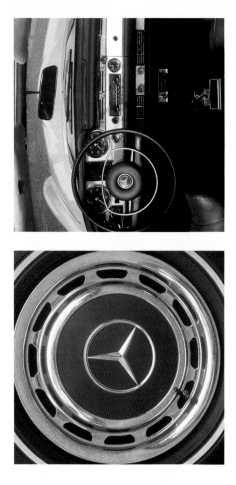

SPECIFICATIONS

Engine	2778cc/169cu.in
Horsepower	170bhp @ 5750rpm
Top speed	121mph (195km/h)
Wheelbase	94in (2350mm)
Weight	2700lb (1224kg)
Sales	23,885

Right: Mechanically, the 1977 Ferrari 308 was little changed, using the same 3.0 liter V8 as the car it replaced, claiming 255bhp in European form (240bhp in less dirty American guise) and a top speed of 140–150mph, depending on the gearing specified.

Left: Not everyone liked the wedge-shaped 308GTB of 1973, but four years later the new 308 looked like nothing else but a Ferrari. Styled by Pininfarina, it had a deliberate resemblance to the first Dinos, with those high front wings and gaping side air intakes. Curves were back, and a Ferrari was a Ferrari once again.

Right: This is a late-model Pantera, but they all followed the same formula of a large, softly-tuned Ford V8 in an Italian chassis. Ford ensured a tight control on costs, so the Pantera was cheaper and less sophisticated than a Ferrari or Lamborghini. But it looked like a true supercar, and even with the 5.7 liter V8 in standard tune, could exceed 160mph. Unfortunately, it was rushed into production, and quality was poor. Ford pulled out after only 4000 cars had been built.

Left: The De Tomaso Pantera was never more than a two-seater, but with a luxurious specification to suit American tastes. Air conditioning was a standard, a specification unheard of in mid-engined sports cars of the time.

Lamborghini Countach

Lamborghini had been first to offer a mid-engined supercar, the curvaceous Muira, which employed a 4.0 liter V12 mounted transversely behind the seats. It caused a sensation, and the Italians knew that its replacement would have to do the same. When it was unveiled in 1971, the Countach did exactly that—even the name was said to be Piedmontese slang expressing astonishment and admiration.

Right: Like a wedge-shaped, V12 powered armadillo, the Countach wasn't beautiful, but was certainly striking. The same 4.0 liter V12 was now mounted fore-aft in a multi-tube chassis, with 375bhp to propel an all-up weight of 3644lb.

Left: As for top speed, no one seemed to know for sure—certainly over 170mph, maybe as much as 190. Unfortunately, this wasn't the right car for the '70s, and the Countach never made Lamborghini's fortune.

SPECIFICATIONS

Engine	3929cc/240cu.in
Horsepower	375bhp @ 800rpm
Top speed	See text
Wheelbase	101in (2450mm)
Weight	3000lb (1360kg)
Sales	1111

Above: A baby Lamborghini? Well, almost. The 1970 Urraco was designed to meet and beat the Ferrari Dino, mid-engined with a 2.5 liter V8 of 220bhp. Both 2.0 liter and 3.0 liter versions followed.

Right: The clever thing about the Urraco's Bertone styling was the way it disguised the car's bulk, plus the fact that it had four seats and was mid-engined. The two-seat Jalpa replaced it.

Lotus Europa

Until the Lotus Europa came along, mid-engined sports cars were exotic, expensive, and invariably Italian. Instead, the little Europa used a 1470cc Renault engine and transaxle, which was well suited to the mid-mounting. This sat in a very aerodynamic bodyshell with a drag figure of just 0.29. So there it was, a miniature mid-engined supercar for just £1100 (the equivalent of $2010)—the ambitious Chapman had been aiming for half that price!

Right: For the 1970s, Lotus dropped the Renault engine in favor of its own twin cam unit, which gave the Europa more Lotus-like performance.

Left: Those "bread van" looks were an aerodynamic ploy, and worked well, but they did seriously restrict rearward vision, an enduring complaint from Europa owners.

SPECIFICATIONS (TWIN CAM)

Engine	1558cc/95cu.in
Horsepower	105bhp @ 5700rpm
Top speed	117mph (188km/h)
Wheelbase	91in (2275mm)
Weight	1568lb (713kg)
Sales	9000 approx

Above: Lotus made a wholesale change in the mid 1970s. The Elan and Europa were dropped, and the Seven sold to Caterham Cars. An all-new Lotus replaced the lot of them, the four-seat Elite (this is the later Excel) which took Lotus into GT territory.

Right: Soon after the new Elite was launched in 1975, the two-seat mid-engined Esprit was unveiled. A truly modern incarnation of the Europa, this used the same 2.0 liter twin cam four that was later turbocharged to great effect.

Lotus Seven S4

Remember the Lotus Seven of the 1950s? it was still in demand 20 years later, but Lotus was determined to make it a little more civilized, and so broaden its appeal to a wider market. The Series 4 Seven, new for 1970, was the result. The diehard Seven enthusiasts were aghast—more room for people and luggage, a comfier ride, even sliding windows! Had the Lotus Seven gone soft?

SPECIFICATIONS (TWIN CAM)	
Engine	1558cc/95cu.in
Horsepower	125bhp
Top speed	110mph (177km/h)
Transmission	4-speed manual
Price	£895 ($1640) kit form
Sales	1000 approx

Left: Just like every other Lotus Seven, this one offered its customers a wide range of engines: Ford 1300 (68bhp) and 1600 (84bhp) plus Lotus twin cam (115 or 125bhp). Performance was vivid.

Left: It might look basic by 21st century standards, but the Series 4 was the most comfortable Seven yet. Four-link rear suspension gave a more forgiving ride.

Below: Updated styling, though still clearly a Lotus Seven. The Series 4 sold well, but the S3 (as a Caterham) outlived it.

Left: The Jensen-Healey, a brave attempt to make a brand new British sports car for the '70s. It looked good on paper (bland styling apart) but the unreliable Lotus engine, and rust problems, put paid to the whole project within three years.

Ferrari Daytona

The fastest production car in the world—quite a title for any car that holds it, and in 1968 the car in question was the Ferrari 365GTB Daytona. Tested at a genuine 172mph, it was slightly quicker than a Lamborghini Muira, while the muscular yet graceful styling by Pininfarina ensured the Daytona's place as one of the Ferrari legends, long after faster cars had come and gone.

SPECIFICATIONS

Engine	4390cc/268cu.in
Horsepower	352bhp @ 7500rpm
Top speed	172mph (277km/h)
Wheelbase	96in (2400mm)
Weight	3530lb (1600kg)
Transmission	5-speed manual

Left: The prancing horse symbol that means so much. As for the Daytona, it came from a line distinct from the little Dino and mid-engined sports cars. Like the 250 GTO, it was a front-engined V12 GT, which meant in Ferrari terms it was relatively heavy.

Above: The Daytona overcame its weight with 352bhp from its four-cam dry-sump 4.4 liter V12. Six twin-choke Weber carburetors allowed it to breathe, and a five-speed transaxle transmitted all that power to the tarmac.

Right: At first, the Ferrari Dino didn't carry Ferrari badges at all—it was a "Dino" pure and simple. The hallowed badges didn't arrive until 1975, perhaps because sales were falling!

Below: By the early 1970s, the baby Ferrari had been upgraded as the 246GT, now with a 195bhp 2.4 liter version of the familiar V6. A cast-iron cylinder block and longer wheelbase made the 246 heavier than the 206 it replaced.

Opposite: This is a hardtop 246GT, but from 1971 Ferrari also offered the targa-topped 246GTS. Targas, with just the central part of the roof removable, became a popular option in the 1970s, when it was thought that full convertibles would be outlawed for safety reasons. Ferrari sold 1270 targa-top 246 Dinos, and nearly 2500 with a full roof. But in 1973, both were dropped to make way for the V8 308. That move signaled the end of Ferrari's V6 period.

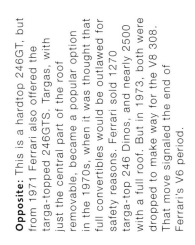

Opposite: In the early '70s Aston Martin desperately needed a new engine to replace its ageing straight six, and it arrived as the company's own 5.3 liter four-cam V8. Complete with fuel injection, it produced around 350bhp, and transformed the performance of the heavy Aston Martin DBS—it was around 20mph faster! But the huge cost of developing its own engine put Aston well into the red.

Left: Lancia had no in-house engine suitable for the Stratos, but Ferrari did. And as both were owned by Fiat, that solved the problem. In Stratos tune, the 2.4 liter Dino V6 produced 190bhp at 7000rpm, and 159lb ft.

Below: The Lancia Stratos was designed, conceived, and built with one aim in mind—to win international rallies. And it did so, being almost unbeatable in the mid-1970s. Not many were used as road cars.

Right: Now this was different. The Matra Bagheera could accommodate three people, the driver and two passengers, so long as they were reasonably friendly.

Below: Mid-engined sports car, French style. The Matra Bagheera came with a choice of 1294cc or 1442cc Simca engines, both enough for a top speed of around 100mph.

Opposite: Last of the traditional Triumph TR series, the TR6 was basically the six-cylinder fuel injected TR5 with a comprehensive restyle by Karmann. A little outdated by the mid 1970s, but this remained the best selling TR of all. Over 94,000 were built in seven years, and 90 per cent of them were exported, most to America. De-rated to 125bhp post-fuel crisis, this was still a fast car.

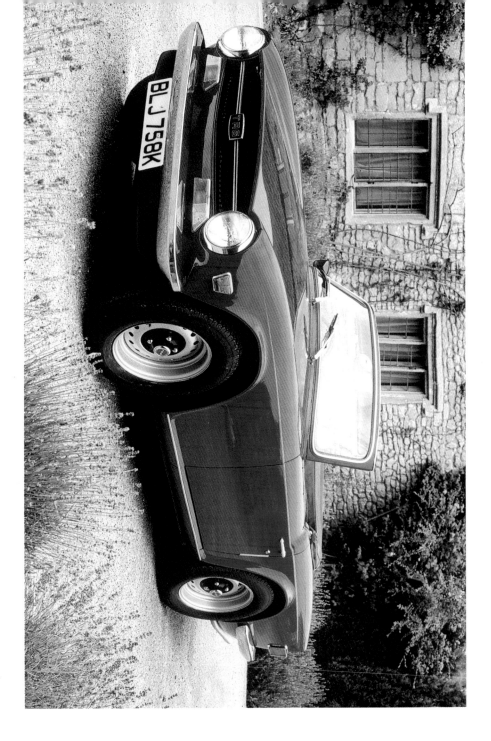

Above: Ford Mustang II—a car of its time. The first fuel crisis was a real shock for America, where gas had always been cheap and plentiful. So for 1974 the Mustang dropped its big thirsty V8s and was radically downsized. Enthusiasts howled, but the car sold well anyway.

Right: Like Ferrari, Maserati maintained a front-engine tradition alongside its mid-engined supercars. This is the Khamsin, a V8 powered 2+2. It took over from the Ghibli, another V8 GT, which came in coupe and convertible form.

Below: Alfa Romeo continued to offer a convertible through the 1970s. This is a Giulietta from the '60s, but the sports car version derived from it, the Duetto, was Alfa's long-lived two-seater.

Right: Datsun's 240Z was upgraded into the 2.6 liter 260Z, though externally it hardly changed. A 2+2 version was added later, along with the 2.8 liter 280ZX.

Right: Porsche wanted a cheaper sports car to slot in beneath the increasingly upmarket 911, and this was the result. It teamed up with VW (which also wanted a sports car) to produce the 914, which used many VW parts to keep costs down, and could wear VW or Porsche badges, depending on who was selling it.

Below: It all looked promising. Mid-engined, the 914 used VW's fuel-injected 1.7 liter flat-four, and while 85bhp was enough for respectable performance, there was still room to fit Porsche's own 125bhp flat-six. Add in a decent amount of room for luggage and two people, and the 914 looked set for success.

Right: Neat details on the 914, but the car never achieved Porsche's target of 30,000 sales a year. Even with all those VW parts, it cost too much to build and sell, though nearly 120,000 did find homes in seven years.

Below: A roomy cockpit was one of the 914's great strengths, along with that removable targa top. And the wheel-at-each-corner layout promised good handling.

Below: Meanwhile, the Porsche 911 carried on through the 1970s in its own inimitable rear-engined fashion. This is the Carrera RS 2.7, offered in 210bhp "touring" specification, or as a stripped-down racer with lightweight bodyshell.

Right: Porsche finally got the entry-level sports car it wanted in the 1975 924. Originally conceived as a VW/Audi (hence the front-mounted, water-cooled Audi 2.0 liter engine) it turned Porsche's traditional layout on its head. This is a later 924 Turbo.

Porsche 928

A decade earlier, it would have been unthinkable—a Porsche with a water-cooled V8, mounted up front. Sacrilege to some when the 928 was launched in 1977, but Porsche had its eyes on a market beyond the enthusiast-driven 911. It wanted to build a high performance GT with wider appeal. This would need to be fast, refined, and with seating for four, but still very much a sports car, and a Porsche, in its responses. The 928, despite its detractors, was just that car.

SPECIFICATIONS (928S)

Engine	4644cc/283cu.in
Horsepower	300bhp
Top speed	155mph (250km/h)
Wheelbase	95in (2377mm)
Weight	3420lb (1550kg)
Sales	10,205 (1979-83)

Below: Porsche needn't have worried. The 928 sold well as exactly the sort of car they wanted to build—a soundly engineered GT that offered a different (but still sports car) driving experience from the 911. The first 928s were in downgraded post-fuel crisis 240bhp form, but were soon uprated to 300bhp and beyond.

Below and right: A comfortable, convenient interior (so long as you liked black). Pictured on the right is the front-engined 3.0 liter 968 of the early 1990s—Porsche's plan to eventually replace the 911 with 928 derivatives never happened.

Below: Lancia has long been the upmarket performance brand of Fiat, as this spoilered show car amply demonstrates. So the 1970s Monte Carlo, originally intended to be a big brother to the successful little mid-engined Fiat X1/9, ended up with Lancia badges.

Right: The Monte Carlo was mid-engined too, powered by a Fiat/Lancia 2.0 liter four-cylinder engine. But Lancia's (and Fiat's) real image builders were always the competition-biased cars such as the four-wheel-drive Integrale.

MGB GT

Already eight years old when the new decade began, the MGB soldiered on right through the 1970s, helped by continuing strong demand for what was one of the last traditional sports cars left in production. Outdated compared to modern coupes and sports saloons, it still offered something that none of those did—that's why it kept on selling right up to 1980.

Left, above, and right: Even in detoxed form, the 1798cc four gave reasonable performance and good economy, while the hatchback GT made a practical sports car. Big black bumpers were essential to carry on selling the MG in its biggest market—America.

NBH 188V

SPECIFICATIONS

Engine	1798cc/110cu.in
Horsepower	95bhp @ 5400rpm
Top speed	106mph (171km/h)
Wheelbase	91in (2310mm)
Weight	2190lb (993kg)
Sales	513,272 (all 4 cyl MGB)

Left: The MGB GT V8, to give its full title, was a fast, compact machine. British Leyland (which now owned much of the British motor industry) fitted the lightweight 3.5 liter Rover V8 to the B GT to produce what it hoped would be a mini-Grand Tourer. The result was 125mph and rapid acceleration, though the V8 wasn't cheap. But crucially, it never qualified for sale in America, a vital market for MG, and without that outlet, less than 2600 V8s were sold before it was dropped in 1976. Rover revived the concept, 20 years or so later, in the open-top MG RV8, using the now fuel injected V8 and a slightly modernized MGB shell. It was a right-hand drive only limited edition, and most of the 2000 RV8s were exported to Japan.

Right: Ferrari joined the mid-engine supercar crowd in 1971 with the 365 BB. "BB" stood for "Berlinetta Boxer," referring to the flat-12 engine, a first for Ferrari.

Below: Despite its looks, the BB had a slightly lower top speed than the front-engined Daytona, owing to less slippery aerodynamics.

Opposite: In 1976, this was the new generation Triumph TR7. Some thought it ugly, but the TR7 was a comfortable sports coupe that sold reasonably well. A convertible and V8 TR8 came late in the day.

Below: In the early '70s, the Chevrolet Corvette was at the peak of its muscle car boom and the top LS6 V8 option offered 425bhp and 475lb ft. That produced a rubber-searing 0–60 time of 5.3 seconds, with 100mph coming up in 12.7 seconds.

Right: The Corvette wasn't seriously downsized in the '70s, unlike other American muscle cars. This is a '78 version, an Indy pace car replica. It was a public relations coup to be picked as pace car for the classic Indy 500 race, so replicas proliferated.

Below: Do all sports cars get fatter with age? That certainly happened to the Datsun 240Z, which started out as a fairly lithe sports car in 1970, but had grown into the touring 280ZX a decade later.

Right: Remember how Colin Chapman sold the rights to the Lotus Seven to Caterham Cars? They made a success of it, and carried on building these back to basics sports through the '70s, '80s, and '90s.

Below: To build the fastest Super Seven yet, Caterham bought-in a Vauxhall 1998cc four-cylinder engine, a 16-valve twin-cam unit that produced 175bhp at 6000rpm. Also available in tuned 250bhp form, it offered blistering acceleration—on the road, nothing short of a big motorcycle was faster.

Below: The Mazda RX-7 was the most successful rotary-engined car ever built. Mazda had finally licked the reliability problems of rotary power, and the super-smooth RX-7 was the proof.

Right: In the 1970s, Alfa Romeo is associated with sports saloons like the little flat-four Alfasud, but it also offered this handsome V8 powered coupe, the Montreal.

THE 1980s

The 1980s saw a sports car revival. Performance was back with a vengeance, but maybe only as a plaything of the rich. Porsche, Ferrari, and BMW all did well out of the '80s boom. Then Toyota launched the MR-2 and Mazda the MX-5—the modern, affordable sports car was back too.

Left: Porsche abandoned plans to replace the 911, and instead developed ever faster, more sophisticated versions.

Below: Old and new. The new Chevrolet Corvette for 1983 (left) was wider and lower than the old car (right) but nine inches shorter and up to 250lb lighter. A 5.7 liter V8 was still the standard power unit.

Opposite: The new Corvette served Chevrolet well, in production for over ten years and selling 40,000 a year through the 1980s. It remained America's one and only home-grown sports car.

Opposite: The '80s Corvette was still powered by General Motors' ageing pushrod "small block" V8, its 5.7 liters offering 205bhp. But for 1990, the radical ZR-1 was unveiled, with a Lotus designed four-cam V8 with four valves per cylinder. That produced 375bhp, enough to propel the Corvette ZR-1 to 175mph, though it was expensive and high maintenance.

Left: The high-tech ZR-1 grabbed the headlines, but the vast majority of Corvettes were sold with the simpler pushrod V8. By the early 1990s this was producing a reliable 305bhp.

Below: The Corvette coupe was popular, but it also came as a full convertible. The pessimists of the 1970s, who predicted that convertibles would soon be dead, had been proved wrong.

Left: While Porsche was penning its front-engined 924 and 928, it had other plans for the 911—turbocharging. The first 911 Turbo appeared back in 1974, giving it instant supercar performance.

Opposite: From certain angles, the 1980s Turbo looked almost identical to any 911 from the previous 20 years, but now packed 3.3 liters and 300bhp. That was boosted again to 330bhp from 1986, enough for 170mph on the autobahn.

Below: Brash, flash, and fast, in some ways the Porsche 911 Turbo typified the get-rich-quick 1980s, preferably in red with a drop top. But it was more lasting than that—there has been a turbocharged 911 ever since.

Above: 911s became more luxurious in the '80s, but they were still sports cars, not GTs.

Right: Look closely, and you can just see the sloping nose of this 935, derived from that of the 935 which dominated Group 5 racing.

Opposite: The 911 was given a ground-up redesign in 1984, and the Carrera of that year was 80 per cent new, with a 3.2 liter version of the flat-six. The whale-tail spoiler was familiar though.

Porsche 959

[I]t might look vaguely like a 911, and still hide a flat-six engine in the tail, but the 959 was a very different car indeed. It was as much a high-tech showcase for Porsche's design skills as a near-200mph road car: electronically controlled four-wheel-drive, six-speed transmission, twin turbochargers, and (on the road car) 450bhp. It wasn't cheap though and only 250 were ever built, but a technical tour de force all the same.

SPECIFICATIONS

Engine	2849cc/174cu.in
Horsepower	450bhp
Top speed	197mph (317km/h)
Transmission	6-speed manual
Weight	2977lb (1350kg)
Sales	250

Opposite: The 959 was originally intended for Group B rallying. It won the Paris-Dakar in 1984. But Porsche had to sell 200 road cars for it to be able to qualify.

Below: Inside this ultimate Porsche looked surprizingly standard, with just a few extra switches.

Left: Funereal all-black interior for the BMW M1. The company made a bigger and more lasting success with the later Z-series sports cars, which used the classic front-engine, rear-drive layout that was expected of BMW.

Opposite: If the Mazda MX-5 was an update of the Lotus Elan concept, then this Toyota MR-2 did the same for the Fiat X1/9. Small and mid-engined, it made use of Toyota's own parts bin to produce a lively, fine handling little car.

Below: With the M1, BMW sought to break into the mid-engined supercar market, until then a virtual fiefdom of the Italian manufacturers. Power came from BMW's own 3.5 liter straight six.

Opposite: There were many replicas of the legendary AC Cobra over the years, but Autokraft's was the most enduring, and received the official Ford seal of approval.

Left: A 1.8 liter turbocharged Nissan engine lifted the Scimitar's performance from so-so to electrifying in this small, light car, with 0–60 in around seven seconds.

Below: A modern British sports car for the '80s? Reliant's Scimitar SS1 used Ford 1300 and 1600 engines for affordable open-top fun.

Opposite: Panther's mid-engined Solo, another Ford 1600-powered sports car, it was not a success.

Right: Bristol survived the '80s by making exclusive cars in tiny numbers. Most drivers had never heard of them.

Left: Bristol Beaufighter, with the famous "100 MPH" registration carried by Bristol demonstrators, which actually understated the performance of this 140mph car. Power still came from a Chrysler V8, now turbocharged, though Bristol refused to quote power and torque figures. How typical of a concern that also refused to advertize!

Ferrari Testarossa

In a decade associated with excess, the Ferrari Testarossa was somehow in keeping. It was intended to combine high speed with cossetting luxury and outrageous looks, and it definitely managed to provide all three in no uncertain terms.

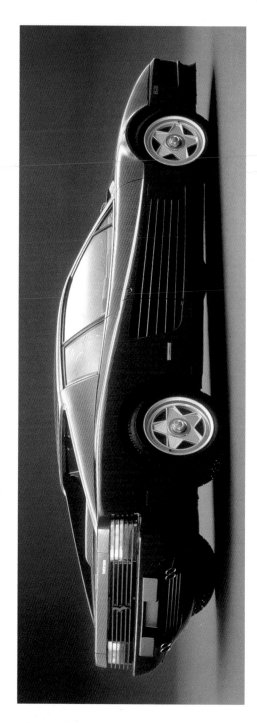

Below: Pininfarinia designed the Testarossa, but those huge side strakes were there for a purpose. The rear-mounted radiators needed intakes that large to keep the latest version of Ferrari's flat-12 cool at 180mph.

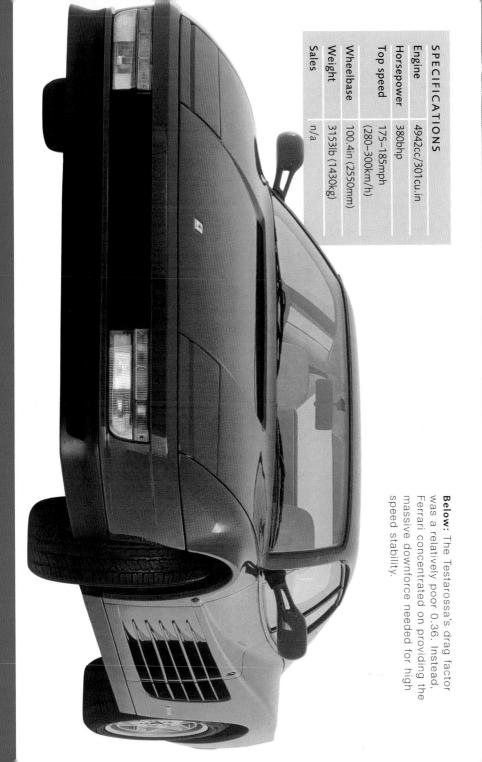

SPECIFICATIONS

Engine	4942cc/301cu.in
Horsepower	380bhp
Top speed	175–185mph (280–300km/h)
Wheelbase	100.4in (2550mm)
Weight	3153lb (1430kg)
Sales	n/a

Below: The Testarossa's drag factor was a relatively poor 0.36. Instead, Ferrari concentrated on providing the massive downforce needed for high speed stability.

Above: The Vector Aeromotive Corporation sought to offer an Italian style supercar, made in America. They chose an authentically Italian 5.7 liter V12 in the 1996 M12. It claimed a top speed of 190mph and 0–100mph in ten seconds.

Right: With the DB7, Aston Martin returned to its six-cylinder roots. Now owned by Ford, it finally had financial stability, not to mention access to production and cost-cutting know-how.

Aston Martin Vantage

The new DB7 launched in 1993 as part of the new Ford-owned regime, was the future of Aston Martin, but through the '80s the Vantage, and the special-bodied Zagato, carried on the big, heavy V8 tradition. Aston Martin claimed better acceleration than a Ferrari Daytona for the Vantage, a power boost of 40 per cent, and a top speed of 174mph. All these claims would prove to be optimistic, but the Vantage served to renew interest in the big, and ageing, Aston.

Below: Suspension made the Vantage handle more precisely than the standard V8, which in the words of one journalist felt like a "vague high performance truck."

SPECIFICATIONS

Engine	5340cc/326cu.in
Horsepower	Not quoted
Top speed	174mph (claimed)
Wheelbase	103in (2610mm)
Weight	3800lb (1727kg)
Sales	n/a

Right: Engines were a problem for the Fiero. The basic 2.5 liter four wasn't powerful enough, and the V6 option introduced a year later was hampered by a four-speed (not five-speed) manual transmission.

Below: Pontiac's mid-engined Fiero looked terrific, though it was intended as an economical commuter with sporting style. As Pontiac management later admitted, maybe it looked too sporty, leading drivers to expect more than it could give.

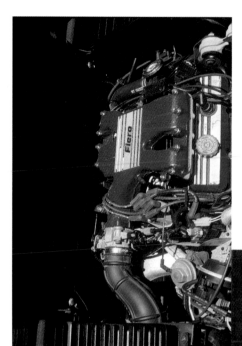

Opposite: Launched in 1984, the Fiero was a runaway success in its first year, with over 136,000 cars sold. GM top management had thought the original forecast of 50,000 units to be wildly optimistic. But sales slumped in 1985, then fell steadily year on year, because of disappointing performance, a series of engine fires, and increased competition. The Fiero was finally dropped in 1988.

Jaguar XJS HE

Jaguar had a problem. The XJS was conceived as a fast, refined Grand Tourer, and did that job superbly well. But its big, thirsty V12 engine drank fuel alarmingly quickly. Too quickly for post-fuel crisis Europe, so the HE ("High Efficiency") XJS arrived in 1983. This used a very high (12.5:1) compression ratio and clever cylinder head design to improve fuel consumption dramatically. It worked, though the XJS would always be a gas guzzler.

Left: High Efficiency maybe, but the XJS remained a well appointed, luxury GT. The automatic-only HE V12 was soon joined by six-cylinder manual and convertible XJSs. Sales soared from just over 1000 in 1980 to over 10,000 by 1988.

Below Left: Fuel injection and the HE package allowed Jaguar's super-smooth V12 to carry on for a few more years.

SPECIFICATIONS

Engine	5343cc/326cu.in
Horsepower	299bhp
Top speed	150mph (242km/h)
Wheelbase	104in (2590mm)
Weight	3859lb (1750kg)
Sales	115,413 (all XJS)

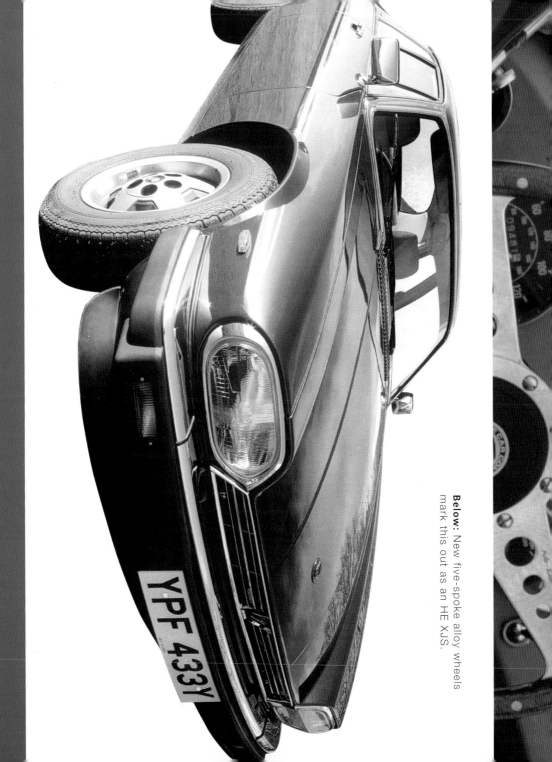

Below: New five-spoke alloy wheels mark this out as an HE XJS.

Above: A sight familiar to enthusiastic drivers for nearly half a century—the dashboard of a Lotus/Caterham Seven.

Left: Caterham Cars bought the Seven design from Lotus in 1973, and they have been building the little cars ever since. They are still based around a tubular spaceframe.

Opposite: Like Morgan, Caterham kept the Seven contemporary by using modern engines, up to a fiercesome 250bhp Vauxhall unit in the HPC. Caterham offered a performance driving package with every HPC sold.

Opposite: To mark its 40th anniversary of building road cars, Ferrari decided to make its fastest road car yet—the F40. Not the most sophisticated Ferrari yet, or the most complete, but the fastest, pure and simple. And with a genuine 200mph, it was.

Below: To achieve that speed, the F40 was stripped down to the basics, and weighed just 2425lb or 500lb less than the high-tech Porsche 959. The 2.9 liter V8 was turbocharged to produce 478bhp at 7000rpm.

Above: Who, passing this car, could not resist a peak through that perspex cover at the most powerful Ferrari road engine ever? The F40 was destined to be gazed at as much as driven.

Left: Pininfarina suggested the F40's basic shape, but many hours were spent perfecting it in the wind tunnel. The monstrous rear wing was there for a practical reason, not for show.

Left: Cadillac had a smart idea in the late 1980s, to combine Italian coach building with American V8 muscle. The Allente was built by Pininfarina on a shortened Eldorado platform. It was then flown across the Atlantic for finishing by Cadillac.

Opposite: The Allente looked every inch a luxury cruiser, though with Cadillac's Northstar V8 in its final year, it performed like a sports car.

Below: Sales were a disaster, at around 3000 a year, and using a 747 to shuttle parts back and forth must have made it hellishly expensive to build. The Allente was dropped in 1993.

Below: Beneath this special paint job lies the most significant sports car of the '80s. With the 1989 MX-5 (or Miata) Mazda managed to recreate the spirit of open cars like the Lotus Elan and MGB.

Opposite: The magic ingredient was to combine that "wind in the hair" feel, and retro looks, with all the reliability, convenience, and ease of driving of a modern car. It was a winning formula.

Below: BMW through and through, the Z1's power unit was the familiar 170bhp 2.5 liter six which already did a good job in the 3 and 5 series.

Opposite: The Z1, sold between 1986 and 1990, was something of a rolling test bed for the Z-axle rear suspension, electric doors, and other features.

Opposite: The Z1 had rather plain, perhaps even dull, styling but its innovative features were far more significant. Electric motors made the doors disappear into those big sills, while the Z-axle rear suspension dramatically improved roadholding over the traditional BMW set-up.

Left: Plenty of BMW styling details helped sell 8000 Z1s in four years. It was followed by the more conventional four-cylinder Z3 and V8 Z8.

Below: The interior was pure BMW, but driver and passenger needed to be quite agile to hop in over those high sills. The Z3 and Z8 reverted to conventional doors.

Below: Sports car, coupe, or super-hot saloon? Who cares, the point about the Audi Quattro was its pioneering use of four-wheel-drive in a performance road car. Street credibility came from rallying success in the forests of Europe.

Right: Audi was in the midst of its five-cylinder period, and the Quattro was powered by a 2144cc overhead cam five, with a turbocharger boosting the output to over 200bhp. But the Quattro will be remembered chiefly for its four-wheel-drive.

Opposite and below: Ford offered a turbocharged Mustang through most of the 1980s, as an alternative to the rorty, back to basics V8. Expensive and high-tech, the Mustang SVO Turbo sold in small numbers. It was really a hangover from the fuel-hungry '70s, when Ford thought it might have to drop its thirsty V8s in favor of more efficient turbo-fours like this one.

Opposite: Alpine was the Porsche of France. At least, that was the aim of Renault, which bought up the little manufacturer in 1974 and helped it launch the GTA in 1984, using the Renault-Peugeot-Volvo 2664cc V6.

Below: Alpines (this is a GTA) were always rear- not mid-engined, which could lead to the sort of tail-happy handling familiar to 911 drivers. But driven below its limit, the GTA was a fast and roomy sports car for two.

Right and below: One day, surely somebody in Hollywood will make a movie out of the DeLorean debacle. John DeLorean was a General Motors high flyer who decided to go it alone. He persuaded the British Government to fund his sports car project, but the DMC12 turned out to be heavy, slow, and a poor seller. Fraud cases followed, and Mr DeLorean ended up in jail.

Opposite: Usually thought of as a 1970s car, but the gem-like Fiat X1/9 was on sale right up to 1989. This was Colin Chapman's vision for the Lotus Europa made real, an affordable, practical sports car with all the handling precision of a mid-engined layout. Starting out with Fiat's 1294cc four-cylinder engine, the X1/9 later upgraded to 1488cc with a five-speed gearbox. Like many Fiats of the time, the X1/9 suffered from rust, but it was delightful to drive. Over 180,000 were sold in 17 years.

THE 1990s

I t was the 1960s all over again. The '90s saw an explosion in sports car choice. On one hand, cars like the McLaren F1 and Ferrari Maranello sought ultimate supercar status. On the other, the MGF, Fiat Barchetta, and new Lotus Elan proved that the affordable sports car was far from dead.

Left: De Tomaso finally abandoned Ford V8 power for the BMW-powered Guara in 1994.

Mercedes 500 SL Roadster

Unveiled in 1989, the new-generation Mercedes SL for the '90s took the concept to its logical conclusion. Safe, reliable, and utterly dependable, but with the same sort of timeless elegance as earlier SLs. And, if you opted for the 5.0 liter V8 or 6.0 liter V12 options, extremely high speeds. They were high-tech, with anti-lock and anti-skid controls, designed to take all the effort and worry out of driving.

Above: That famous three-pointed star was as valued a status symbol as ever, but one reason that celebrities often chose the SL was for its understated looks.

Left: Just as important to buyers spending a large five-figure sum, the SL was about as well put together as a car could be. Owners could be certain that every electronic gadget would work faultlessly, and carry on doing so for years.

Above: An automatic flip-up roll bar (if the car turned over) was standard, as was a power hood.

SPECIFICATIONS	
Engine	4973cc/303cu.in
Horsepower	326bhp
Top speed	155mph (250km/h)
Wheelbase	100.6in (2515mm)
Weight	4010lb (1918kg)
Sales	n/a

Above: This was one of the most luxurious sports cars available.

Right: The wide choice of power units include six or eight-cylinder 2.8, 3.0, 3.2, or 5.0. The 6.0 liter V12 came along later.

Opposite: The SL retained a family resemblance to previous compact Mercedes, even back to the original 190SL of the '50s.

Below: Not exactly graceful, but then the Alfa Romeo SZ was never intended to be any such thing. Alfa commissioned Italian house Zagato to design and build an arresting, controversial coupe—so they did.

Right: The limited edition SZ (just 1000 coupes were made, plus a further 800 convertibles) was based on Alfa Romeo 75 saloon parts, which brought a 3.0 liter V6 engine and five-speed transaxle.

Opposite: Launched in 1993, the six-cylinder DB7 was a result of the new well-financed Ford era at Aston Martin. Like many '90s sports cars, its retro styling sought to suggest an earlier era.

Below: Jaguar's bid for the ultimate supercar was the XJ220. They claimed 210mph for the mid-engined twin-turbo V6, and testing proved that to be accurate. Only a McLaren F1 was faster. This is the TWR racer.

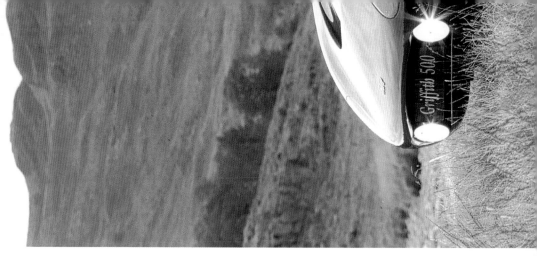

Below: Tiny TVR from Blackpool not only survived independently into the 1990s, but thrived. This Griffith combined a sleek, elegant body with V8 power.

Right: Everyone admired the Griffith's style, and underneath was a sophisticated, competent road car, developed by a tiny team of engineers.

Opposite: The 1990s Griffith still used a highly developed 3.9 or 4.3 liter version of the ex-Rover, ex-Buick pushrod V8, which had left its original drawing board 30 years earlier. It did the job.

Below: Ex-Lamborghini employee Claudio Zampolli had a dream to outdo not just Lamborghini, but Ferrari and Maserati as well. The Cizeta V16T looked like the car to do it with.

Opposite: Zampolli's creation was striking looking, but all attention was on the V16 engine, the first 16-cylinder unit offered for decades. Said to have been developed from two Ferrari V8s spliced together, the 6.0 liter unit made use of two radiators, eight camshafts, and 64 valves. It was mounted transversely, explaining why the Cizeta was 80mm wider even than a Ferrari 512BB.

Right: Unlike many such dream cars, the Cizeta actually made it to production, and a claimed 520bhp promised true supercar performance. But the dream lasted only three years, and just 20 Cizetas were built.

Below: This was Honda's pitch at building a Ferrari. The NSX had an exotic aluminum monocoque and four-cam V6, but was also easy and convenient to drive. What it lacked was snob-appeal.

Right: British kit car manufacturer Ginetta survived against all the odds, offering a variety of fiberglass bodied cars based on mass production parts. This is the G33, with Ford Zetec or Rover V8 engines.

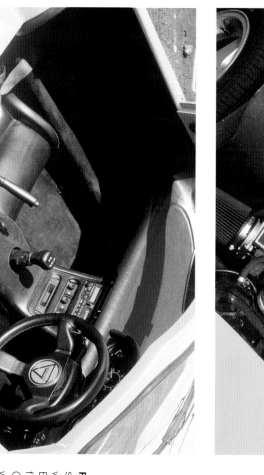

Left and below: The ubiquitous Rover V8, a favorite of so many British sports car manufacturers, endowed the lightweight G33 Ginetta with stunning performance. Originally designed by Buick back in the early '60s, it was still burning rubber 40 years later. The Ginetta's interior was typically plain and businesslike.

Right: Ginetta toyed with more modern shapes in the 1980s and '90s, notably with the wedge-shaped G25 and G32. Both were Ford powered and the former was mid-engined. But the curvy G33 came along at the right time, when retro styling was in and Ginetta was poised to take full advantage of its 1960s racing heritage.

Left, above, and right: The Lotus/Caterham Seven spawned numerous look-a-likes over the years and this Westfield was one of the most successful. This Rover V8-engined Seight had the unrivaled power/weight ratio of 400bhp/ton, and rocketed from 0–100mph faster than a Lamborghini Countach or Porsche 911 Turbo. Westfield also fitted a Ford 1.8 liter turbo-diesel, which combined good performance (0–60mph in 6.6 seconds), with 50mpg!

Left: From this angle, the only clue as to the Seight's thunderous V8 power unit is those foam air cleaners poking out of the bonnet. Top speed was limited by aerodynamics to around 140mph, but the Seight could whip from 50–70mph in just 2.5 seconds.

Above: Some enthusiasts scorned the Nissan Z-series, especially in later ZX guise. Not real sports cars, they said, too big, too soft, too heavy. Maybe, maybe not, but the bottom line was that Nissan were selling more Z-cars than ever before (around 70,000 300ZXs a year). Smooth riding, convenient and comfortable, but with 300bhp from its twin-turbo V6—North America remained its biggest market.

Left: The last Bugatti was built in 1951, but 36 years later a consortium bought up the name and announced plans to produce an all-new Bugatti supercar, fit for the 21st century. Unveiled in 1990, the EB110 GT lived up to the promise, a V12 mid-engined sports car with four-wheel-drive. And making the most of that evocative name, it was finished in traditional Bugatti blue. A brand new factory was built in Modena, Italy, and the EB110 finally staggered into production in 1993. But only 98 cars had been completed before bankruptcy loomed. Plans for an EB112 high performance saloon came to nothing. The Bugatti name was later bought by VW.

Right: The Super Sport EB110—EB110S—was the sports racing version, stripped down to cut weight and with an extra 40bhp squeezed out of the V12. It also had a fixed rear wing, rather than the standard car's wing which retracted into the body at lower speeds.

Chevrolet Corvette ZR-1

Chevrolet had an ambition—to make the Corvette the fastest production car in the world. Faster than Ferrari, Porsche, or Jaguar, this was a flagship that was aimed at bringing glory to General Motors. Could they do it?

Left: Its secret weapon was an all-new aluminum V8, designed for the Corvette by Lotus (now a GM subsidiary). Four cams, 32 valves, and sequential fuel injection.

Opposite: Despite its exotic hardware, the ZR-1 looked very much like any other Corvette.

SPECIFICATIONS

Engine	5736cc/350cu.in
Horsepower	375bhp @ 6000rpm
Top speed	178mph (287km/h)
Wheelbase	100.4in (255.0cm)
Weight	3465lb (1575kg)
Sales	5890

Left: The ZR-1 had the paper specification to match its Lotus-designed V8, including stiffer springs, adjustable damping, a six-speed gearbox, and ultra-low profile tires. It needed all of that to cope with the engine's 375bhp and 370lb ft.

Below: But was it really the fastest production car in the world? *Road & Track* timed one at 178mph, so maybe not. Still, it was cheaper than a Ferrari, and even at twice the price of a standard Corvette, was almost a performance bargain.

Below: The fourth generation Chevrolet Camaro was launched in 1993. It stuck faithfully to the V8 rear-wheel-drive formula, but now it had organic '90s styling, and better handling.

Right: The world might have moved on by the 1990s, but Ferrari still offered a mighty, front-engined V12, a four-seat Grand Tourer with the emphasis on the driver. This new 456 was launched in 1992.

Below: At 5.5 liters, the V12 under the 456's bonnet was Ferrari's biggest road engine yet. Whether mated to a manual or automatic transmission, it endowed the big GT with stunning performance.

Opposite: Was the big front-engine layout outmoded? Not according to Ferrari, which in 1996 dropped the Testarossa in favor of the 550 Maranello, which was a two-seater 456 capable of 199mph.

Right: This is the fastest sports car of all time, and it will probably never be surpassed. Formula One race car designer Gordon Murray was given carte blanche in laying out the McLaren F1. No restrictions on costs or materials—this was to be the ultimate supercar. So when the F1 was unveiled in 1993, maybe we shouldn't have been quite so surprised by the figures: 231mph (leaving other 200mph cars like the Ferrari F40 far behind); 0–60mph in 3.2 seconds; 6.0 liter V12 of 627bhp (built by BMW especially for the car); six-speed manual gearbox; carbon bodyshell; list price, £540,000, equivalent to $993,920 (or for the race-spec, but road-legal LM, £799,000, or $1,470,630). Yet there was no high-tech four-wheel-drive, traction control, or even ABS—the F1's aim was to bring a full-blooded race car experience to the road. The trouble was, by the time it came to market, the world was in recession, and many of the mega-rich who had put down deposits on the fastest car in the world decided they couldn't afford one after all. Four years later, McLaren pulled the plug on the whole project, after just 100 cars had been built. In an uncertain world of finite resources, it's unlikely we will see a car like the McLaren F1 ever again.

Opposite: The De Tomaso Pantera (nearly 20 years old by now) was given a substantial revamp in 1990 by Marcello Ghandini, with a cleaner, softer look, though it was still clearly a De Tomaso. The boss and founder of the marque persevered with the car even after Ford pulled out, selling around 100 a year right through the 1980s and early '90s.

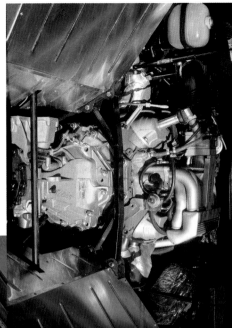

Left: Under Ford's influence, early Panteras used a 5.7 liter Ford-built pushrod V8 in virtually standard trim, though later cars were boosted to 350bhp.

Below: Panteras were always luxurious by supercar standards—air conditioning was standard. This betrayed their aim of selling to American customers. The combination of top-level trim, a reliable Ford V8, and Italian style was seen as a perfect combination.

Opposite: From 1992, the Dodge Viper sought to recreate the spirit of the AC Cobra, employing a massive engine in a small lightweight body with simple steel chassis. In a word, it did.

Below: The Viper's 8.0 V10 was based on a truck unit, though built of aluminum and with fuel injection, and it was tuned to the eyeballs (to use an old motoring cliche) for a raucous 400bhp.

Ferrari 355 F1

Below left: No turbo, but the 355 pushed out 380bhp. Five valves per cylinder and an 8500rpm red line were part of the reason.

Once, a 3.0 liter V8 was the small Ferrari, for those who didn't need (or couldn't afford) a top speed of over 180mph. The F355 changed all that. With a "mere" 3.5 liters it could top 185mph and gave a driving experience second to none. The open-top Spider was icing on the cake.

Below: Strictly a two-seater, the 355 was very much a driver's car, with pin-sharp steering and controlled, supple suspension—a more useable car than a Testarossa.

SPECIFICATIONS	
Engine	3498cc/215cu.in
Horsepower	375@8250rpm
Bhp/liter	107bhp/liter
Transmission	6-speed manual
Top speed	183mph (295km/h)
Acceleration	0-60mph 4.6 seconds

Left, above, and right: This particular 355 has the Formula One option, a semi-automatic gear change controlled by Formula One style "paddles" either side of the steering wheel. This electro-hydraulic set-up did away with the clutch, allowing the driver to choose between four modes: normal, sport, auto, or "low grip" (allowing for optimum traction on snow or wet conditions).

Left: These were the last few years for Porsche's air-cooled flat-six, before it was replaced by an all-new water-cooled six in 1997. That would have nothing in common with the old one except its basic layout. In basic 3.4 liter form, it produced 296bhp; as a 3.6, make that 320bhp. Adding a turbo (which Porsche did in 1999) boosted power to 420bhp. For the ultimate new 911, the almost race-ready GT2, that was 455bhp, enough for 0–60 in just over 4 seconds, and a near-200mph top speed.

Opposite: This 1991 Turbo was thought to be outdated by some, even as it was launched. Why? Well it just missed out on Porsche's new six-speed gearbox, not to mention the four-cam flat-six engine of the new Carreras. It did have a new chassis and bigger turbocharger, while retaining the familiar 911 shape. So this particular 911 was an odd mixture of old and new—later cars were more complete.

Left: A break with tradition. The De Tomaso Guara, unveiled in 1993, was the first De Tomaso not to use a Ford V8. After 30 years of fidelity to Ford, Alejandro De Tomaso chose a 4.0 liter BMW V8 to power his all-new sports car for the '90s. It used BMW's six-speed gearbox as well.

Below: Unfortunately, putting the Guara into production was a great strain on De Tomaso's resources. The man himself was ill, and was forced to sell his interests in Maserati and Moto Guzzi motorcycles to support the new car. But he succeeded, and the BMW-powered Guava went on sale.

Below: Mercedes SLK, a smaller version of the SL concept—K stood for "Kurz", or short in German. And the SLK really did feel like an SL in miniature, a solidly built roadster, strong on safety features.

Right: Unfortunately, it turned out to be a little too like the low-powered SLs, and in early 2000 Mercedes dropped the basic 2.0 liter four-cylinder engine, offering instead two supercharged versions (163 and 197bhp) plus a 218bhp V6.

Below: Intense rivalry between Lamborghini, Ferrari, and Maserati kept all three on their toes. So the new Diablo was a clear shot across Ferrari's bows. Crucially the Diablo claimed 492bhp, more than an F40.

Right: Not just more power than an F40 or Testarossa, but the option of four-wheel-drive as well. Lamborghini was benefiting from the financial and technical support of Chrysler, which now owned the company. Later Diablos had a 6.0 liter V12 offering 550bhp.

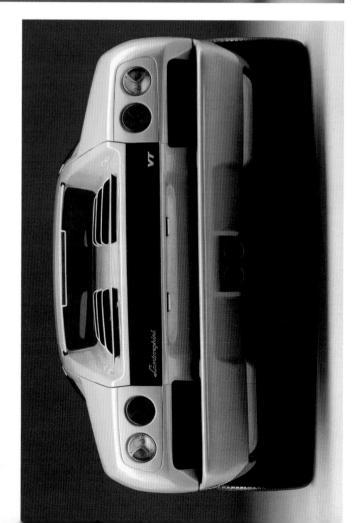

Left: Based on the XJS platform, but the new XK8 2+2 was a far more shapely (and Jaguar-shaped) sports car. Jaguar's sports car for the '90s sold far faster than its predecessor, thanks to its curvaceous shape and four-cam V8 engine.

Below: Kit car made good. The evergreen Marcos was reintroduced in 1981, and moved ever upmarket in the '90s, employing a Ford-USA four-cam V8 in the Dennis Adams designed shell, which had been launched back in 1964. Production ceased in 2001.

Below: Back to basics for Lotus in the 1990s. Despite corporate troubles (Proton was the company's third owner in a decade) Lotus managed to design, prove, and productionize the lightweight, mid-engined Elise.

Opposite: The Elise moved away from Lotus' upmarket aspirations of previous years. Interior trim was basic, and the whole package aimed at pared to the bone weight, excellent handling, and driver appeal. Power came from Rover's 1.8 liter twin-cam K-series.

Above: The Vanquish succeeded in boosting Aston Martin back into the supercar league. The six-cylinder DB7 was all very well, pretty, popular, and no doubt profitable too, but it wasn't the ultimate image booster that Aston needed. The Vanquish V12 was.

Right: The DB7 was a real success for Aston Martin, selling 7000 cars in its first ten years. In 1999, this Vanquish V12 was launched, claiming 190mph from its 460bhp 6.0 liter V12. The body was an alloy-bonded monocoque.

Below: Maserati Shamal, the final incarnation of the Biturbo, a compact luxury saloon unveiled back in 1982. In a move away from the company's supercar base, it used a 2.0 liter V6 with twin turbochargers.

Opposite: The Biturbo V6 was later upgraded as 2.5 and then 2.8 liters, giving more Maserati-like performance. Dated by 1993, it was updated as the Shamal that year, the same year, incidentally, that Fiat took over Maserati, finally giving it financial stability

Above and above right: A 200mph speedometer was maybe a little optimistic for the Shamal, but it was still a quick car, thanks to Maserati's own four-cam 32-valve V6 engine.

Below: A dream car for British patriots? The Bentley Hunaudieres wasn't quite the rebirth of Bentley's racing spirit as it seemed. With underpinnings from the Lamborghini Diablo VT, and powered by a VW-built W16 of 620bhp, it was most definitely an international effort.

Opposite: One of the great survivors, Alfa Romeo's Spider was in production for 27 years, from 1966 to 1993. The combination of Pininfarina's elegant bodywork and zesty twin-cam power was the secret.

Below: The Spider (called the Spider Duetto for the first few years of life) was always an unashamed two-seater. Alfa Romeo preferred to make civilized room for two rather than cram in four small seats.

Below: At the front, the Spider had changed little in 27 years, an indication of how right the original design was. But its long rear tail was shortened in 1970, and given an abrupt cut-off in '82.

Opposite: Final versions of the two-seat Alfa did away with the 1980s spoilers, and looked better as a result. Towards the end of its life, the Spider sold almost exclusively in America, where it had a big following. By this time, a 2.0 liter twin-cam with fuel injection had been standardized, giving up to 126bhp—plenty for lively open-air motoring. In the '70s, Alfa had reintroduced the 1600 and even offered a little 1300, the Junior Spider.

Opposite: It wasn't just the British who built Lotus Seven replicas. Joop Donkervoort of Loosdrecht, near Utrecht in Holland, did too. His Donkervoort S8AT was intended to be modern, comfortable, and user friendly. All-round independent suspension gave a reasonable ride, and the soft top was said to be waterproof at 100mph on the autobahn! Twin fuel tanks gave a maximum range of nearly 250 miles.

Left: Engine of choice for the Donkervoort was a four-cylinder 2.0 liter Ford, with a Garrett T3 turbo and intercooler—complete with catalyst, that allowed for 170bhp and a 0–60 time of 4.8 seconds.

Below: Low, eager, and ready for the road. The Donkervoort might be more convenient than the original Lotus Seven, but it gave much the same driving experience, seating the pilot just inches from the ground.

Below: Not much room for luggage in the MGF's front end, but there was another compartment behind the rear-mounted engine. This was the first-ever production mid-engined MG, and a practical one.

Opposite: MGF was the first MG sports car in over a decade. Attractive styling, Rover's modern K-series engine (in 1.8 liter 118bhp or 146bhp forms), plus of course the hallowed MG badge, made it a winner.

Below: One unique feature of the MGF was interconnected Hydragas suspension, which used gas in place of conventional steel springs. It provided a good ride and handling, and was transferred directly from the Rover 100 hatchback (formerly the Metro).

Above: Realizing the value of the MG badge, Rover made sure it was prominent. The MGF was based around Rover saloon components, just as every other MG sports car had been. It was an honorable (and economic) tradition.

Opposite: It might look like another MGF, but this is the Lotus Elan for the 1980s and '90s, the first front-wheel-drive Lotus ever, and the first to come with a Japanese engine (a 1.6 liter twin-cam Isuzu).

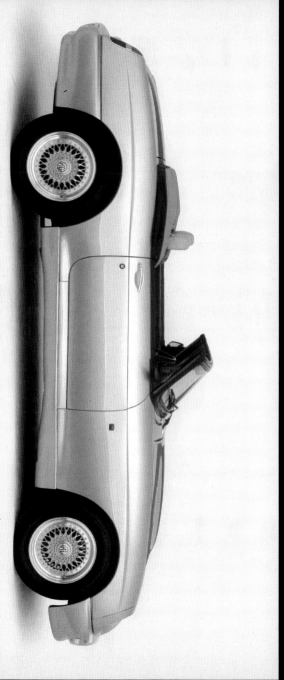

Opposite: No retro sports car. This was the real thing. The MG RV8 was a substantially revamped and updated MGB for the 1990s, a limited edition special to renew interest in MG in preparation for the new MGF.

Below: MGB bodyshells were already being built for the thriving spares market, but the RV8 was updated with flares and sills, not to mention the venerable Rover V8, here in 190bhp 4.0 liter form.

THE 2000s

So could the sports car face the 21st century? It certainly looked that way, with new exotica from new names like Pagini, Mosler, and Noble. Morgan reinterpreted its age-old theme with the Aero 8 while MG, Mazda, and BMW took care of the entry-level end. And Mercedes went back to the future.

Left: The US-built Panoz Esperante was powered by a Ford-USA V8 of 4.6 liters, straight out of the Mustang.

Below: Porsche's new entry-level sports car for the 21st century, the Boxster. Not exactly cheap, but less expensive than a 911, and still fast enough to be fun, with a 2.5 liter (later 2.7 liter) oil-cooled flat-six.

Right: This was the first road-going mid-engined Porsche. The 911 carried on its time honored rear-engine way, while the 944/968 series was always front-engined. Being mid-engined meant it gave the Boxster near-perfect 48/52 weight distribution.

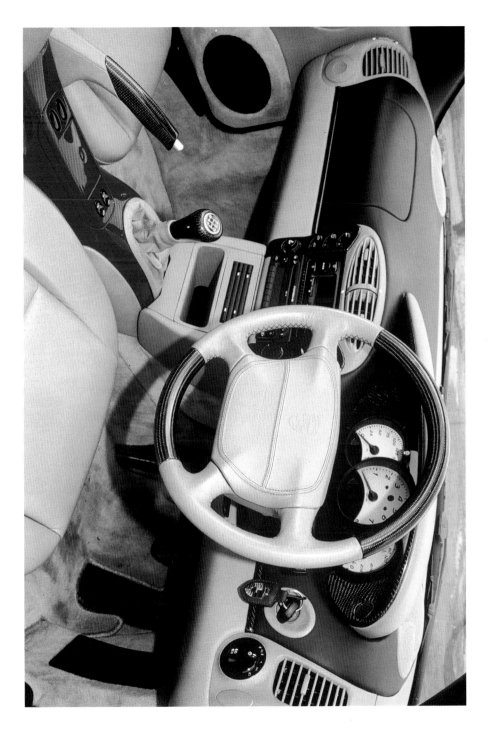

Left: Pilot's view from the TT, Audi's compact little sports coupe launched in 1998. Despite the use of VW Golf components, it wasn't cheap, but it made use of Audi's expertise in turbocharging, five-valve cylinder heads, and four-wheel-drive.

Below: Audi also offered a convertible TT, with the same running gear as the coupe. That meant 225bhp from the 1.8 liter four-cylinder 20-valve engine, providing the driver with agile, eager performance.

Below: Confirmation that sports cars in general, and open-top sports cars in particular, were back in fashion. Audi had shown no interest in pure sports cars for years, but the TT made clever use of existing VW and Audi components to create their unique little coupe (or convertible) though it wasn't cheap.

TVR Cerbera

TVR had humble beginnings in the British kit car market. Later it specialized in rorty two-seaters powered by the Rover V8. But the Cerbera was different. It was the biggest TVR yet, the long wheelbase making it a 2+2, and under the bonnet was TVR's very own all-new V8, the AJP8. It was astonishing that a company the size of tiny TVR managed to finance, commission, and produce its own engine, but it did.

SPECIFICATIONS

Engine	4475cc/273cu.in
Horsepower	420bhp @ 6750rpm
Top speed	200mph (320km/h) claimed
Wheelbase	101in (2570mm)
Weight	2600lb (1100kg)
Sales	n/a

Left and right: The Cerbera (named after the three-headed dog of Greek mythology) opened up a new market for TVR, not just in its seating and size, but in sheer performance. The narrow-angle 75-degree AJP8 looked unexciting on paper, with only two valves per cylinder and a single overhead cam per bank of cylinders. But in 4.5 liter form, it made the Cerbera quicker to 100mph than a Dodge Viper GTS.

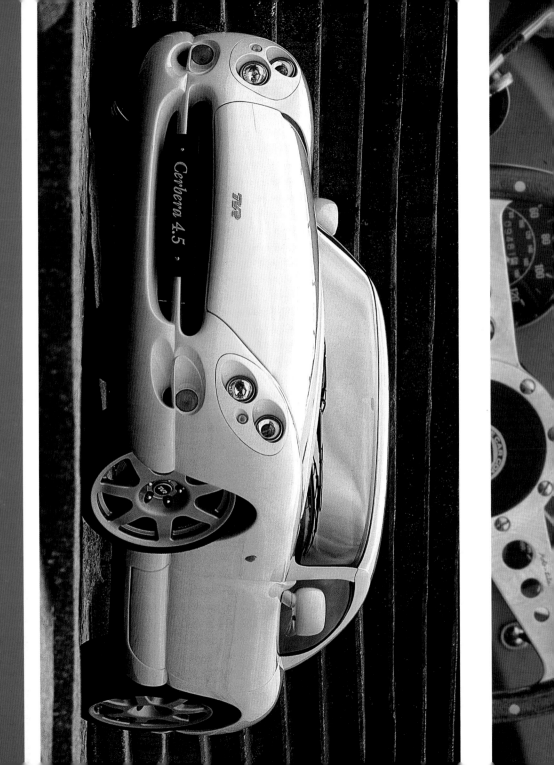

Left: Having a standard coupe hard top was something else that made the Cerbera different from traditional open-top TVRs. These later shared its AJP8 power unit.

Below: Truth be told, the Cerbera was pretty cramped transport for four people, but the 2+2 layout did add adaptability to what was still a stunningly quick sports car.

Left and below: Not as avant garde as the original Z1, the V8-powered BMW Z8 harked back in character to BMW's 507 of the 1950s. Like that, it was designed as a characterful two-seat sports car, with performance and driving experience as its top priorities. Using BMW's own 4.9 liter 400bhp V8, top speed would have been around 180mph, had it not been electronically limited to 155. Nought to 100mph was dispatched in 11 seconds.

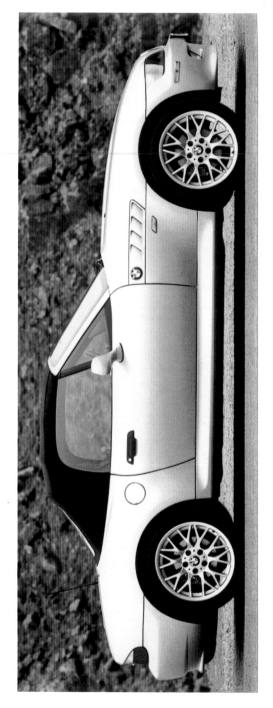

Above: Now owned by VW-Audi, Lamborghini continued to offer a V12 mid-engined supercar in the Italian tradition. As ever, the spur was to outdo Ferrari, so the new Mercielago boasted Lamborghini's biggest, most powerful engine yet, a 6.2 liter V12 of 571bhp.

Above: A more cossetting, airbag equipped, interior than those of early Lamborghinis. Underneath the luxury trim, four-wheel-drive was standard (carried over from the Diablo), as was ABS and a six-speed manual gearbox.

Right: Revitalized by Fiat/Ferrari ownership, Maserati dropped the ageing Biturbo/Shaman in favor of a new generation of front-engined cars, the V8 coupe and (shown here) the Spyder. For the latter, Maserati's V8 was enlarged to 4.2 liters and 385bhp.

Below: Into the 21st century, and Mazda still carried the torch for rotary engines. Its range of rotary-powered saloons of the 1970s sold reasonably well, but it was the RX-7 sports car that proved a real long-term success.

Right: The RX-8, which was announced at the 2001 Detroit Motor Show, was the RX-7's long awaited successor, powered by a 250bhp 1.3 liter rotary engine of very compact dimensions. To improve handling, it was mounted "front-midship."

Left: The Panoz Esperante borrowed many of its components from the Ford Mustang Cobra, and that included the instruments, in an unusual center-dash pod. In Cobra tune, the four-cam V8 produced 320bhp at 6000rpm and 315lb ft. The transmission, brakes, and suspension were all Cobra too.

Left: Using so many Ford parts was a deliberate attempt to keep the price down. Don Panoz (who until then had only ever built racecars) expressed the wish that he wanted to build an "affordable" supercar.

Far left: The Esperante was intended as a home-grown all-American alternative to the Mercedes SL or Jaguar XK8, though the curvy aluminum bodywork (designed by DZN of California) provided that authentically Italian look.

Right: In road going MT900S form, the Mosler supercar had air conditioning, electric windows, power-assisted steering, and anti-lock brakes. At $200,000, it had to pamper as well as exhilarate.

Below: Modern technology was blended with aerospace engineering in evolving the mid-engined Mosler MT 900 model, which used a 5.7 liter Chevrolet engine. Although the Mosler was an all-American creation, many of its styling cues were Italian.

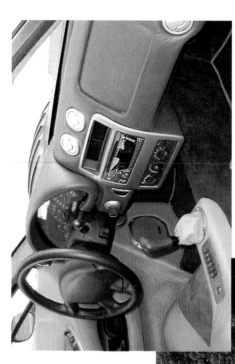

Opposite: The Chevrolet Corvette may have been America's only home-grown sports car for a while, but not any more. Florida millionaire Warren Mosler lent his name to the Mosler MT900, which was designed on cyberspace then bolted together as a prototype— everything fitted, first time out. Not a Corvette rival, but the MT used many Corvette parts, including a tuned version of the familiar V8, here in 5.7 liter 425bhp form.

Pagani Zonda

So was the supercar dead in the 21st century? Not a bit of it. As well as the new American marques, Pagani hailed from Modena in Italy, home of the hyper sports car. Smaller than Ferrari or Lamborghini (with a corresponding budget), Pagini bought-in a V12 from Mercedes and eschewed complexities such as four-wheel-drive.

Right: According to some, the Zonda's hour-glass figure was influenced by that of Horacio Pagini's wife, while the whole car was a tribute to his friend, the legendary Argentian racing driver Jean-Manuel Fangio.

Left: A distinctive rear end, like no other supercar, dominated by the fixed rear wing (unusual in 2003) and those four big tailpipes. The Pagani Zonda was almost brutal from some aspects, hour-glass figure or not!

SPECIFICATIONS

Engine	7291cc/445cu.in
Horsepower	555bhp @ 5900rpm
Top speed	220mph (354km/h)
Wheelbase	106in (2730mm)
Weight	2756lb (1250kg)
Sales	n/a

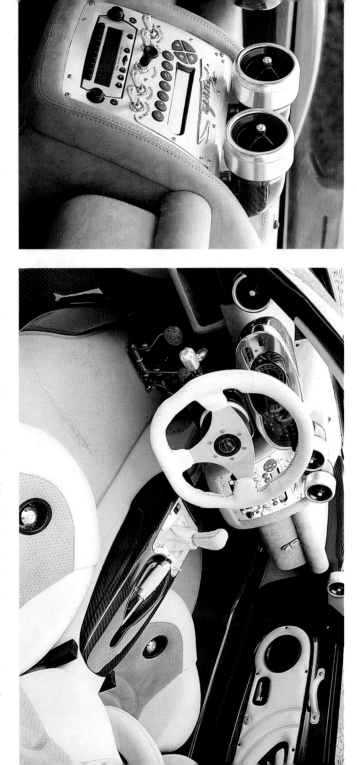

Left: Instead of developing his own engine, Pagani bought the Mercedes V12, an AMG-tuned version displacing 7.3 liters. The massive 60-degree V12 engine was aspirated and relatively low revving compared to the V8s or 12s from Ferrari and Lamborghini. Peak power arrived at 5900rpm, but at 555bhp it wasn't lacking.

Above and above left: Not hugely luxurious or spacious for two, and the only concession to high-tech driver aids was traction control. Zonda drivers had no ABS or four-wheel-drive, though they probably wanted it that way.

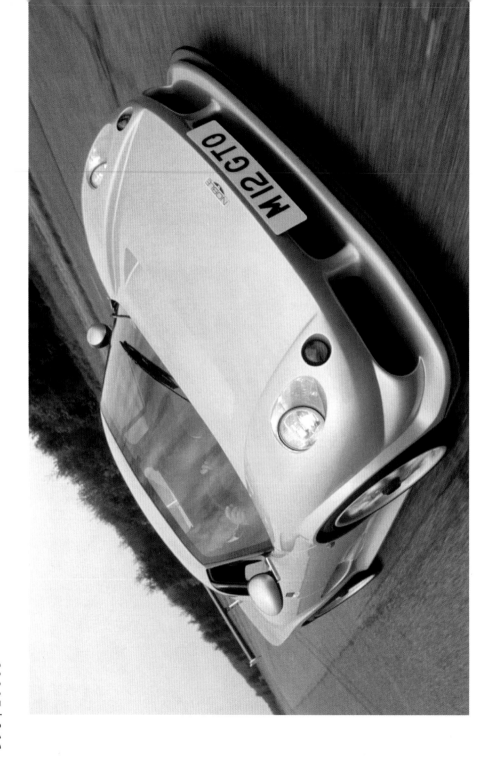

Left: Starting with a fairly mundane engine, the 2.5 liter Ford Mondeo V6, Englishman Lee Noble designed a mid-engined sports car capable of 150mph. The V6 sat transversely behind the seats, with its five-speed gearbox, and with twin turbos was boosted to 310bhp at 6000rpm. Not modern supercar figures, but with a low claimed weight of 2161lb the Noble M12 promised near-supercar performance.

Right: Serious looking kit. Lee Noble had also designed the chassis of the McLaren F1, so he brought a good track record to the drawing board. The M12 did without fancy, high-tech weight saving materials, instead utilizing a steel multi-tube spaceframe and steel bodywork, which made that all-up weight all the more impressive. Nor was there ABS, traction control, or four-wheel-drive—so was this a McLaren F1 in miniature?

Left and above: Fast becoming an American legend, the Dodge Viper celebrated 10 years in production with a mild restyle. Underneath, the faithful 8.0 liter V10 still packed a considerable punch—450bhp at 5200rpm, enough for 192mph in the highest of six gears.

Right: Sacrilege! The first all-new Morgan ever, the Aero 8 had an aluminum bonded chassis, ABS, power steering, modern suspension, and a 4.4 liter BMW V8. But it still looked like a Morgan.

Left and above: In an age when high-tech retro captivates the imagination, Mercedes' SLR (inspired by the original gullwing SLR of the 1950s) was perhaps inevitable. Announced at the 2003 Frankfurt Motor Show, it captured headlines as well.

Right: Why? Well there was the all carbon fiber construction, the supercharged 5.5 liter V8 with 626bhp and 576lb ft. There were swing-wing doors (recalling those '50s gullwings) ceramic brake discs, and an air brake. Top speed—a mere 209mph.

Index

Left: Was there ever a purer expression of the sports car spirit? The original Lotus Six was noisy, uncomfortable, and inconvenient...but great fun.

Picture Credits

Andrew Morland © copyright

Front cover and pages: 28-30, 37, 51, 54, 80, 84-85, 87-88, 90-93, 105, 112-115, 120-124, 128-129, 131-133, 137-142, 157-159, 164-167, 171-179, 186-187, 191, 197, 200-201, 204, 208, 214-217, 219-221, 228-229, 235, 238-241, 254, 256-259, 262, 266-267, 284-285, 288-292, 305-307, 309-314, 316, 323-325, 328-329, 332-335, 338-339, 344-347, 350-352, 358-363, 393.

Garry Stuart © 301

The publisher wishes to thank the organizations listed below for their kind permission to reproduce the photographs in this book. Every effort has been made to contact the copyright holders for permission, however we apologize if there are any unintentional omissions. In case of any omissions please contact Salamander Books Ltd.

Pictures Courtesy of Aston Martin © 104, 130, 134, 263, 300, 348-349

Pictures Courtesy of DaimlerChrysler © 394-395, 340-341

Pictures Courtesy of Alfa Romeo UK © 298, 299

Pictures Courtesy of Honda © 308

Pictures Courtesy of Automobili Lamborghini © 342-343

Pictures Courtesy of Mazda © 278

Pictures Courtesy of Volvo Car UK Ltd. © 70